CULTURA IN
3.º ANO

CULTURA IN
3.º ANO

Meet Alex and Carla	Page 4	An introduction to the Natural Science course characters		
Meet Ana and Tom	Page 5	An introduction to the Social Science course characters		
❶ **Living things**	Page 6	**COMIC** A trip to the beach	**SCHOOL TRIP PROJECT** Living and non-living things concept map	
❷ **Community**	Page 20	**COMIC** A trip to the town centre	**SCHOOL TRIP PROJECT** Road safety poster	
❸ **Where we live**	Page 34	**COMIC** A trip to the city centre	**SCHOOL TRIP PROJECT** Map of the city centre	
❹ **Time and history**	Page 46	**COMIC** A trip to the history museum	**SCHOOL TRIP PROJECT** Old and modern objects table	
❺ **Matter, materials and mixtures**	Page 60	**COMIC** A trip to a recycling plant	**SCHOOL TRIP PROJECT** Properties of recyclable materials poster	
❻ **Energy**	Page 74	**COMIC** A trip to an eco-house	**SCHOOL TRIP PROJECT** Mains electricity and batteries Venn diagram	
Picture dictionary	Page 86	Key vocabulary		

CONTENT • A world of living things • Life processes of animals and plants	• We classify living things into subgroups • Living things adapt	**FIND OUT** Plants need sunlight	**THINK ABOUT IT** Help each other	**LOOK BACK** Study skills: concept map and classroom vocabulary bank Review of Unit 1
CONTENT • Family and school • Local government	• Road safety	**FIND OUT** Make a leaflet about where you live	**THINK ABOUT IT** Celebrating community	**LOOK BACK** Study skills: concept map and sticky notes Review of Unit 2
CONTENT • We live in different places	• Areas of a city	**FIND OUT** How to make a bar chart	**THINK ABOUT IT** Protect your local monuments	**LOOK BACK** Study skills: concept map and maps on the internet Review of Unit 3
CONTENT • Time and history • Periods of history 1	• Periods of history 2	**FIND OUT** Timelines	**THINK ABOUT IT** Traditions from the past	**LOOK BACK** Study skills: concept maps and learner types Review of Unit 4
CONTENT • Matter changes • Mixtures	• Where do materials come from?	**FIND OUT** More about mixtures	**THINK ABOUT IT** Different materials, different uses	**LOOK BACK** Study skills: concept map and revision with images Review of Unit 5
CONTENT • Different types of energy	• Sources of energy	**FIND OUT** More about thermal energy	**THINK ABOUT IT** Saving energy	**LOOK BACK** Study skills: concept map and question-and-answer cards Review of Unit 6

Meet Alex and Carla

1 Answer Carla and Alex's questions.

Hello! I'm Carla. I'm eight years old. I love art and making things. What do you like doing in your free time?

Hello everybody! I'm Alex. I'm eight years old too. When I grow up I want to be a scientist. What do you want to be when you grow up?

2 Unscramble the words and say what Carla and Alex like.

Carla likes ..... .

a i g n t i n p

u n a t e r

Alex likes ..... .

n r e a g d i

a n m i a s l

Meet Ana and Tom

① Answer Ana and Tom's questions.

Hello! I'm Ana. I like finding out about different people and where they live. Where do you live?

Hello! I'm Tom. I like looking after the Earth. What can you do to help look after the Earth?

② Match these objects to Ana and Tom's clues.

A   B   C   D

1. I use this to learn about different countries and oceans.

2. I use this to find out what direction I'm going in.

3. I use this to look at the stars.

4. I use this to measure the temperature.

5

1 Living things

There are living things and non-living things all around us. We can classify anything on the planet into these two groups. Living things are born, they grow, they reproduce and they die. They need oxygen, food and water to live. Non-living things can be natural or man-made.

1. Find some living and non-living things in the picture.

2. Name some man-made things in the picture.

3. Find some natural, non-living things in the picture.

4. Who is not behaving properly in the picture?

5. Listen to the song. Copy the words in the order you hear them.

people

car

plant

boots

water

animal

A trip to the beach

1 🔊 **Listen and read.**

A
"Carla, come here quickly! I can see lots of living things!"

Alex and Carla are exploring some rockpools...

B
"Look, that fish is moving towards that plant."

"Are you sure it's a plant? I think it has tentacles... and a mouth!"

C
"It's eating the fish!"

"Ahhh! That's not a plant!"

D
"You're right, Carla. It looks like a plant, but it's an animal. It's a sea anemone."

2 🛡 **Look at the story. Write one or two words to complete the sentences.**

1. Alex and Carla are on a trip to the ..... .

2. Carla and Alex are investigating a rock pool. Clara can see non-living things: she can see sand, rocks and ..... .

3. Alex can see lots of living things: he can see fish, a crab and a ..... .

beach

pebbles

sea anemone

Alex and Carla's school trip project

Look at Alex and Carla's project, then answer the questions.

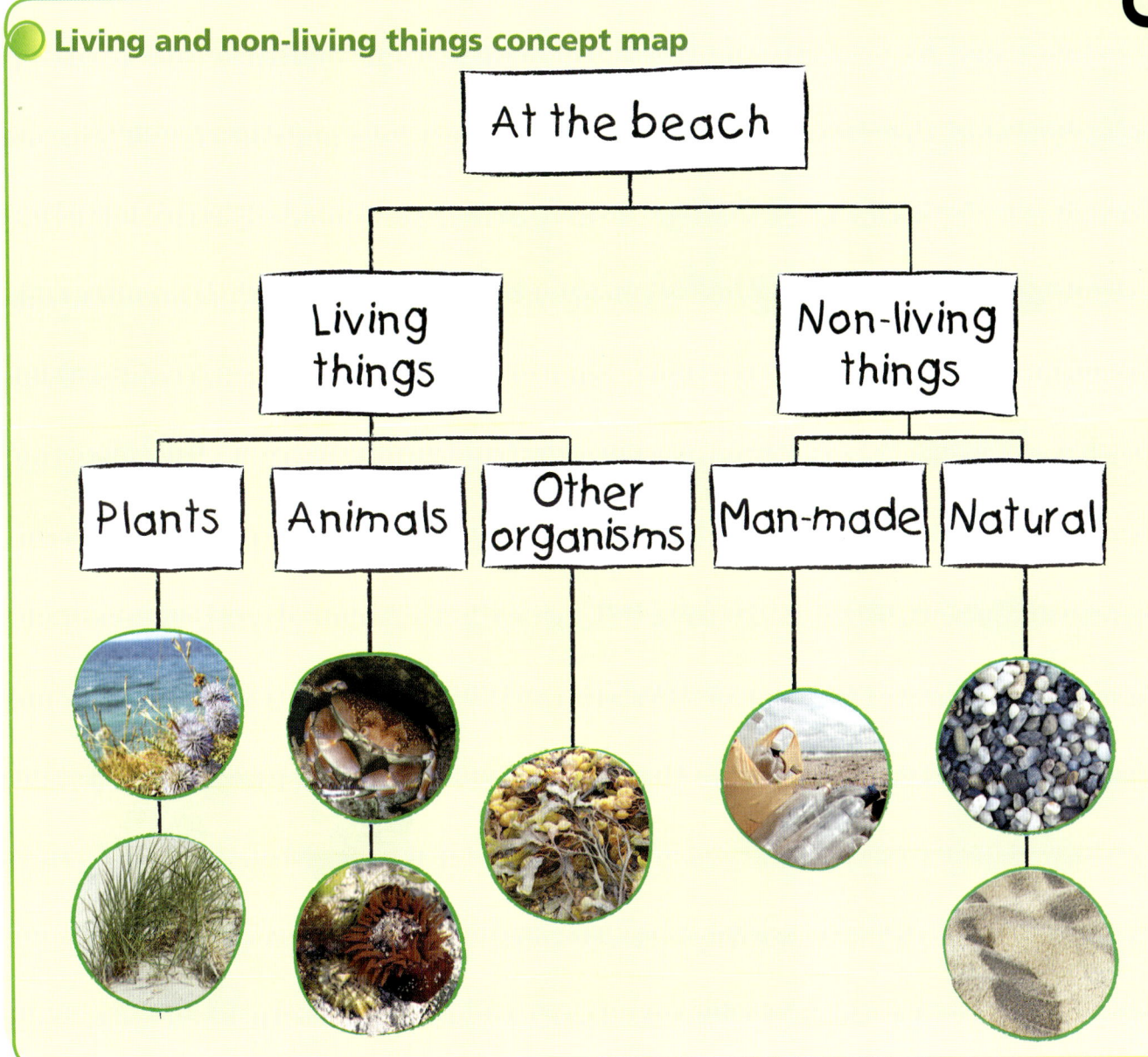

1. Copy the chart. Add another thing from the beach to the categories *animals* and *man-made things*.

2. Carla wants to add the word *driftwood* to the chart. What does it mean? Where does it go?

3. Look at the living things in the chart. Write down some characteristics they have in common.

A world of living things

You already know that animals and plants are **living things**; can you think of other types of living things? Look at the pictures below and discover three other types of living things.

1. Trees are plants.

2. Frogs are animals.

3. Mushrooms are fungi.

4. Cactuses are plants.

5. Snails are animals.

6. Seaweed is algae.

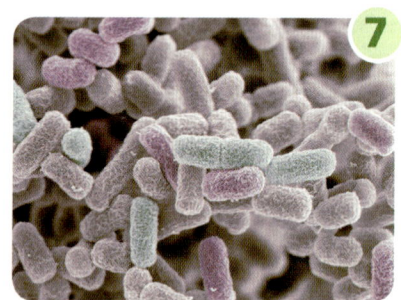
7. *E. coli* is bacteria.

Did you know?
One of the oldest living things on Earth is *Posidonia oceanica*. It is a type of Mediterranean seagrass. It could be more than 100 000 years old!

1. What type of living things do you think Carla is looking at? Explain your ideas.
2. True or false: mushrooms and seaweed are plants.

Classifying living things

We classify living things into **different groups**. To do this we identify similarities and group similar things together. Look at the fact files to find out more about living things.

Animals

- Feed on other living things.
- Can move. Most animals can move from one place to another.
- Can be oviparous or viviparous.
- Have senses.

Plants

- Produce their own food.
- Can't move from one place to another, but can move towards light or water.
- Plants are born from seeds or spores.

Fungi

- Feed on other living things that are decomposing.
- Can't move.
- One example is mould.
- More similar to animals than plants.

Other organisms

- **Algae** produce their own food but have different parts to plants. One example is seaweed.
- **Bacteria** are very small organisms. We can only see them under a microscope.

3 Classify these living things: toadstool, grass, potato, butterfly, salmonella. You can use the internet to help you.

4 What grows on food when we leave it for a long time? How do we classify it?

Life processes of animals and plants

All living things carry out these life processes: **nutrition**, **reproduction** and **interaction**. Let's have a look at how plants and animals carry out these life processes.

Nutrition

Living things obtain **nutrients** from food. Nutrients help them to grow and function properly.

- Animals do not make their own food. Some eat meat, some eat plants and some eat meat and plants.
- Plants use sunlight, water and nutrients from the soil to make their own food.

Reproduction

Living things reproduce. Reproduction means **making new living things**.

- Some animals give birth to live young and others lay eggs.
- Most plants reproduce by making seeds that grow into new plants. Some produce spores.

Link it up

Look at the picture on the right and identify the different parts of the plant. Name at least four.

Now look at the main picture. Can you identify the different parts of the plants in it?

Interaction

Living things interact. **Moving**, **touching** and **communicating** are examples of interaction.

- Animals move, communicate and react to the world around them. Some animals live in groups and some animals live alone.

- Plants also react to their environment. They grow towards the light and their roots grow towards water. Some plants open and close, and some plants can climb.

Did you know?

Some plants have sensitive leaves. The *Mimosa pudica* plant closes its leaves when we touch them.

1. Find three oviparous animals in the pictures.
2. Think of different ways animals interact.
3. Investigate carnivorous plants and climbing plants. You can use the internet to help you. Present your work using ICTs.

We classify living things into subgroups

Plants have similarities and differences

Living things from the same group have similarities and differences. Identifying these helps us to classify living things from the same group into different **subgroups**.

One way of classifying plants is by looking at their **stems**. This helps us to classify them into three subgroups: **grasses**, **bushes** and **trees**.

oak tree

pine tree

Grasses have a soft stem. They are thin, flexible and usually short.

Wheat is a grass. It has a long stem and many kernels at the end of each stem. We make bread from wheat.

Bushes have woody stems with low branches. They are taller than grasses and live longer.

The **blackberry bush** has lots of long branches. These branches have thorns. The fruit is called the blackberry.

Trees have a thick, woody stem called a trunk. The branches grow out from the trunk, high above the ground.

- **Deciduous trees** lose all their leaves in autumn. **Oak trees** are deciduous.
- **Evergreen trees** produce leaves all year round. **Pine trees** are evergreen.

1. Use the following words to classify the plants in the pictures: *deciduous, evergreen, tree, grass, bush, fruit, cones, kernel, stem*.

2. Find examples of different plants in your local area. Find out the names of the plants. Use the words from activity 1 to classify them.

14

Living things adapt

Amazing changes

The **first living things** appeared on our planet over 2 000 million years ago! Can you imagine what these living things looked like?

Over time, living things have **changed** and **evolved**. This has created the variety of life on our planet today.

Look at the incredible plants and animals in the pictures below. Read about how they have changed over time to **adapt to their environment**.

Fossils tell us what living things looked like millions of years ago.

Brown bears have adapted to low temperatures by hibernating during the coldest months of the year.

Cactuses have adapted to have thick skin so they don't lose water in hot and dry environments.

Stick insects have adapted to look like their environment so other animals can't see them.

1. When did living things first appear on Earth? How do we know what they looked like?

2. Match the words to make sentences.

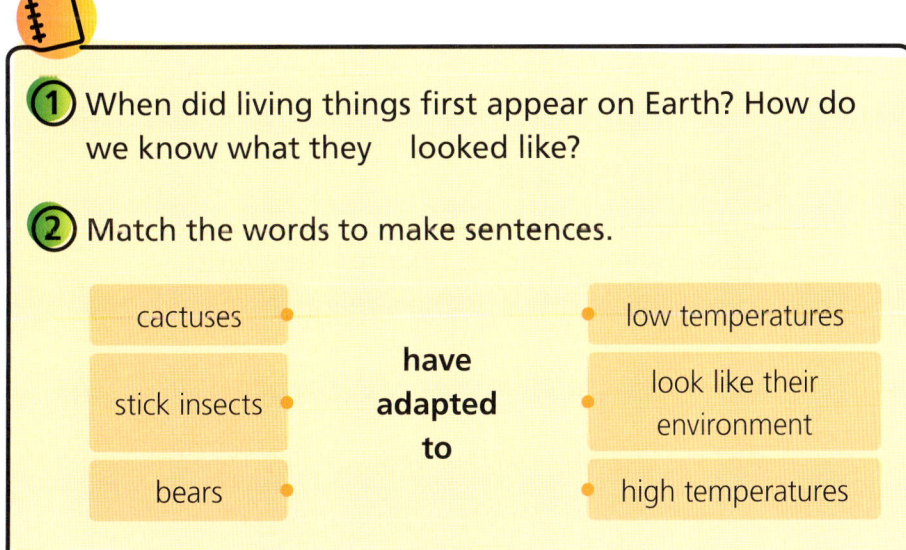

Did you know?

Some wild animals have adapted to live in towns and cities. In the UK, foxes sometimes enter urban areas to look for food.

FIND OUT: Plants need sunlight

Idea:
Plants move towards sunlight.

- Plants in pots
- Camera
- Notebook
- Pencil

Test:
Observe if plants move towards sunlight.

1 Put the plants near the window, facing away from the sunlight.

2 Observe how the plants move towards the light.

3 Take photos and record how the plants move in your notebook.

Conclusions

① How long does it take for the plants to move towards the sunlight?

② Do all the plants grow at the same speed?

③ Display the results of your investigation in the classroom. Use the photos to show how the plants moved.

THINK ABOUT IT: Help each other

A perfect match

You already know how important it is for us to help each other and to look after the environment, but did you know that other living things help each other too?

Look at the pictures and guess how the living things work together. Use the key words to help you.

- blackbird
- eat
- seed
- tree
- plant reproduction

- ox
- oxpecker
- eat
- clean
- insects

- shark
- pilot fish
- parasites
- protection

1. Write sentences about how these animals work together. Use the key words to help you.

2. How do bees help plants reproduce? Search for information on the internet, then present your ideas using ICTs.

17

LOOK BACK: Living things

Study skills

1 Copy and complete.

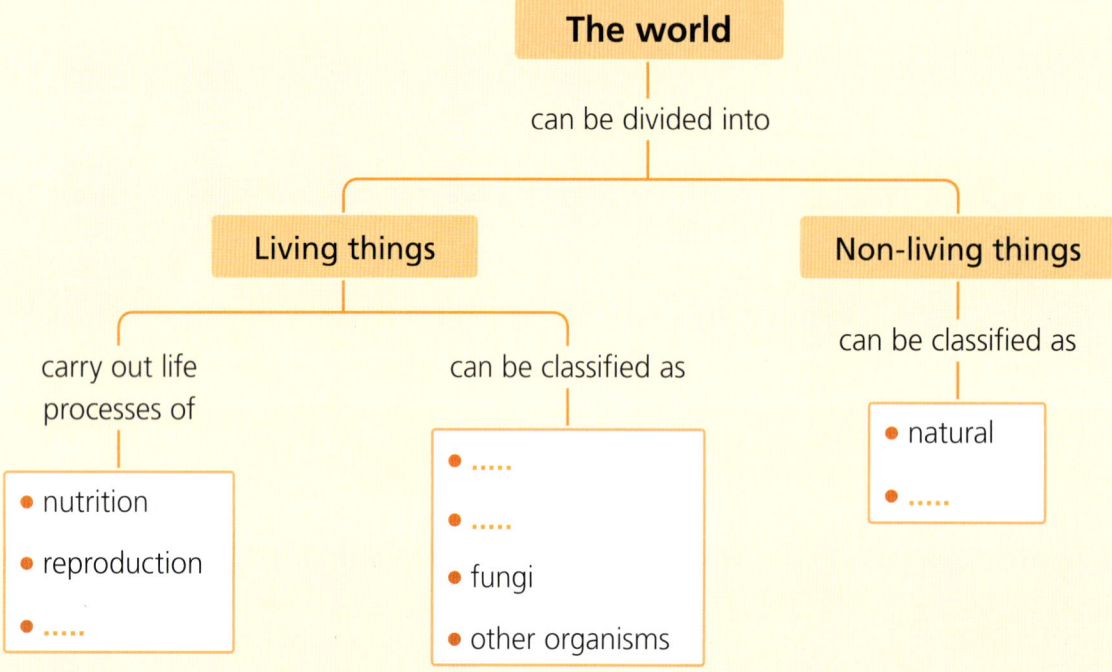

2 Make a classroom vocabulary bank.

- Use paper from the recycling bin. Fold and cut the paper into eight pieces.
- Look through the unit and choose eight important words.
- Draw a picture of each of them. Put them in a plastic slip or a box. Do this for all the units of the book.
- Test each other at the beginning of every class. Choose a picture and describe it. Your partner has to guess the word.

Start today! Find eight important words from Unit 1.

Review

1 True or false? Copy the sentences and correct the ones that are false.

a. Animals, plants and rocks are living things.

b. Reproduction is one of the life processes of non-living things.

c. Non-living things can be natural or man-made.

d. Communication is an example of nutrition.

e. Shrubs and grasses are types of fungi.

2 Classify these living things.

 A
 B
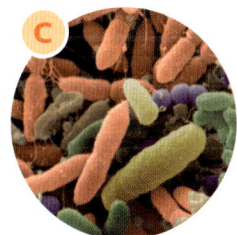 C
 D
 E

3 Identify these life processes.

 A
 B
 C
 D
 E

4 Work in pairs. Order the questions and test your partner.

Pupil A

a. do / food / make / own / their / animals?

b. is / plant / a / mushroom / a?

c. lay / do / horses / eggs?

d. climb / can / plants?

Pupil B

a. is / plant / seaweed / a?

b. do / plants / food / make / own / their?

c. are / viviparous / animals / snakes?

d. is / pebble / a / thing / living / a?

19

2 Community

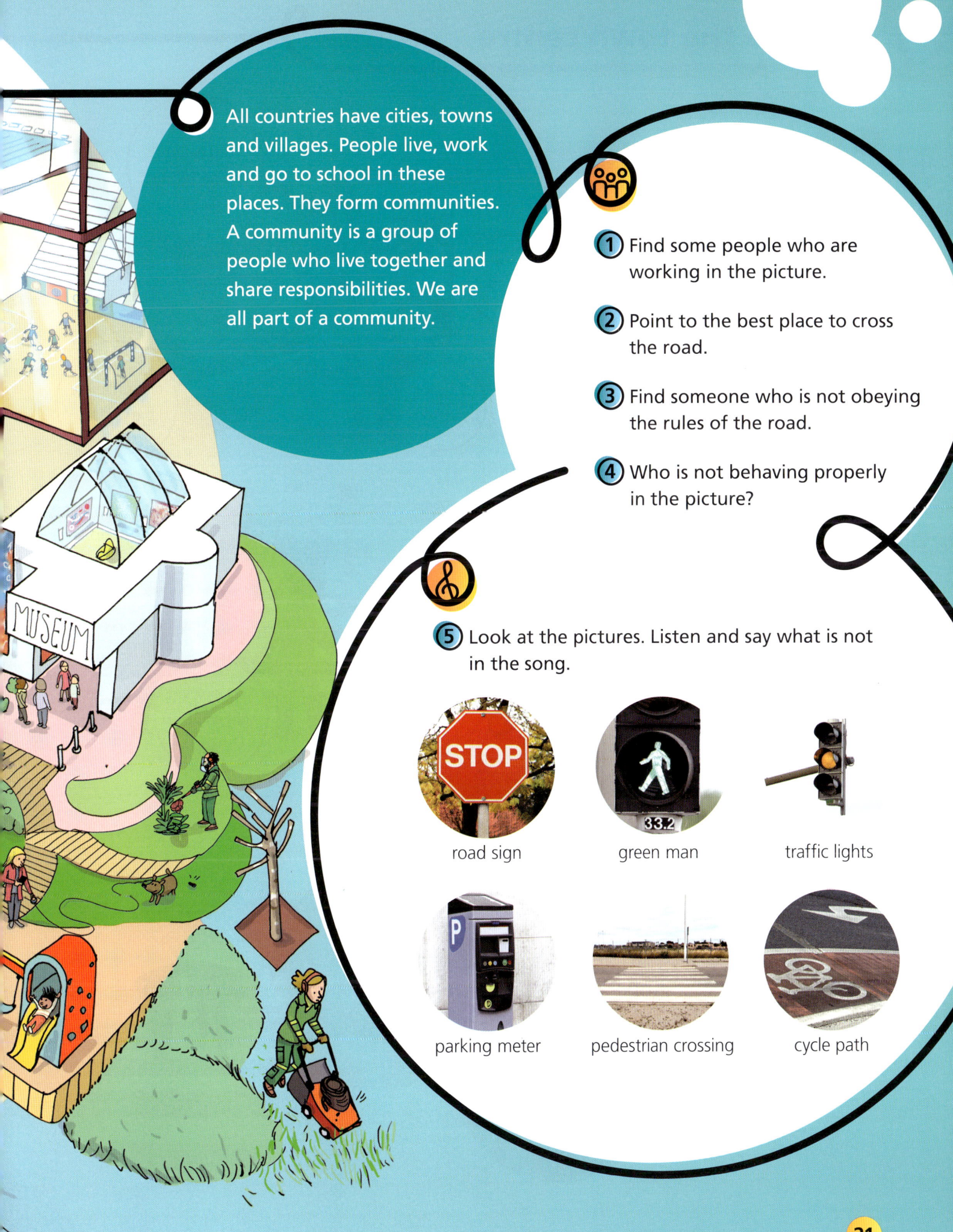

All countries have cities, towns and villages. People live, work and go to school in these places. They form communities. A community is a group of people who live together and share responsibilities. We are all part of a community.

1. Find some people who are working in the picture.
2. Point to the best place to cross the road.
3. Find someone who is not obeying the rules of the road.
4. Who is not behaving properly in the picture?

5. Look at the pictures. Listen and say what is not in the song.

road sign

green man

traffic lights

parking meter

pedestrian crossing

cycle path

A trip to the town centre

1 🔊 Listen and read.

A Ana and Tom are learning about road safety ...

- Oh no, Ana! We're behind the rest of the class.
- Let's cross the road here.
- Wait, don't cross! We're still behind you.

B Never cross the road between two parked cars. It's dangerous!
- Why is it dangerous?
- Because it's difficult to see the vehicles on the road.

C There's a cycle path here too!
- I didn't notice that!
- Bikes are just like cars. We have to look out for them at all times.

D The best place to cross the road is at a pedestrian crossing.
- You have to wait for the green man.
- And look left, right and then left again!

2 🛡️ 🔊 What is the police officer describing? Listen and write it in your notebook.

22

Ana and Tom's school trip project

Look at Ana and Tom's project, then answer the questions.

● **Road safety poster**

① Copy the poster in your notebook. Add two more ways we can be safe when we are walking around town.

② What protection should we wear when we ride a bike? What about skateboarding and roller-skating?

③ Use the internet to find out what the *green cross code* is. Write down the steps and draw pictures to help you explain it.

Family and school

Family

A family is a group of people who live together and take care of each other. How many people are there in your family?

All families are different

Every family is unique and special because all families are different.

- Some families have **one or two children** and other families have **lots of children**. Some families have children that are **adopted**.

- Some families have **two parents** but other families **only have one**. Sometimes another family member, such as a grandparent, **acts like a parent**.

Families can look different but all families love and respect each other.

Family responsibilities

Each member of a family has important responsibilities.

- **Parents** protect, love and teach their children so they can grow up happy and healthy. They work to pay for a home, food and clothes.

- **Children** have an important role in the family too. They respect and listen to their parents. They go to school and can help out at home with tidying up, cooking and washing the dishes.

1. Why is every family unique and special?
2. List the responsibilities of parents in a family.
3. Name eight people you can find at a school.

Link it up!

Animals can also be members of a family. We must love, protect and respect our pets.

24

School

We spend a lot of time at school, so it's important that we all respect each other and make school a happy place where we all can learn. The people in a school can be divided into two groups: **pupils** and **staff**. The pupils are the children that attend school, and the staff are the adults that work there.

The **head teacher** manages the school. The **deputy head teacher** helps the head teacher manage the school.

Different **teachers** teach different classes.

The **secretary** works in the school office.

The **caretaker** and the **cleaners** look after the school buildings.

The **cooks** prepare lunch and sometimes breakfast too.

The **supervisors** look after the pupils during break times.

④ What responsibilities do you have at home? Write a list and compare with your partner.

⑤ In groups, list your school rules. Discuss these rules and order them from most important to least important.

Local government

Most people live in villages, towns and cities. Every village, city and town has its own **local government**. The group of people who work in the local government is called a **town council** or **city council**. The head of the council is called the **mayor**. These people are the leaders of the town or city. They work together to manage and take care of the local community.

The council and the mayor work in a building called the **town hall** or **city hall**. They have meetings and make important decisions about local laws, services and taxes.

Every four years there are **local elections**. All the adults in the community can vote for people to be on the council. The mayor is chosen by the members of the council.

Examples of public services

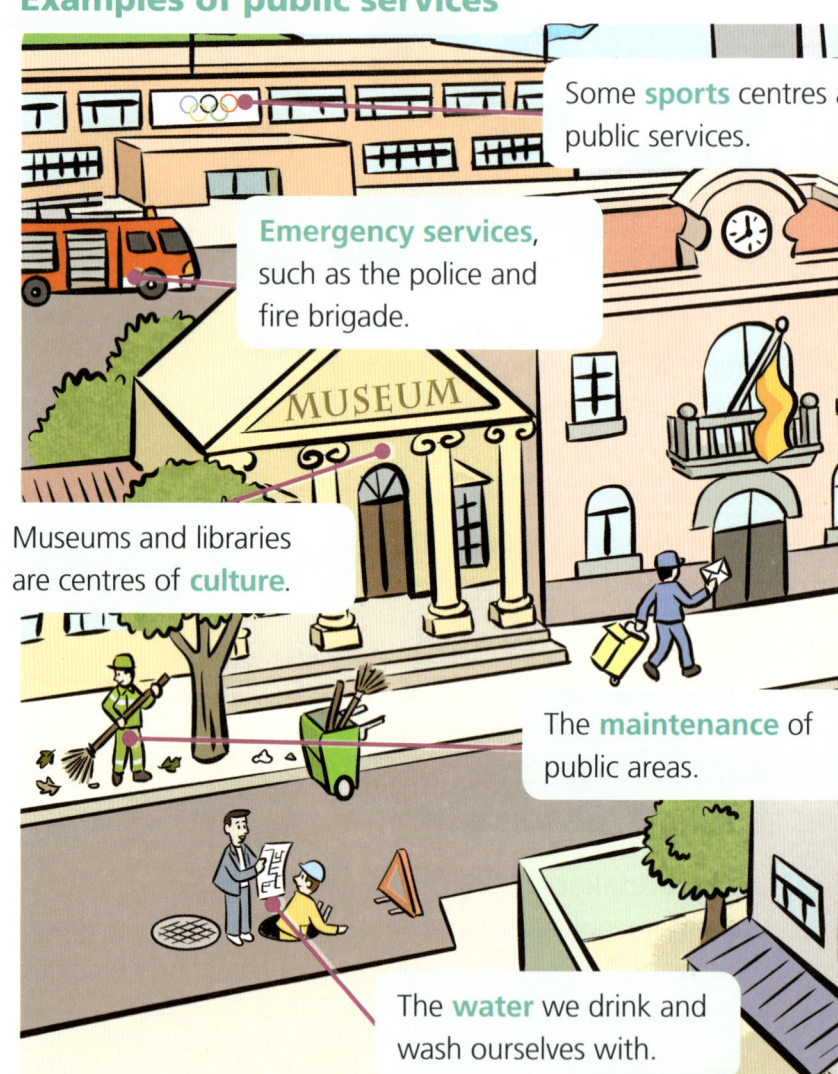

Some **sports** centres are public services.

Emergency services, such as the police and fire brigade.

Museums and libraries are centres of **culture**.

The **maintenance** of public areas.

The **water** we drink and wash ourselves with.

① Write definitions for these words: *town / city council, town / city hall, mayor*.

② Why do people pay taxes?

③ Explain what the police and fire brigade do.

Public services

People pay **taxes** to the local government. Taxes are money that is used to pay for **public services**, such as the police, the fire brigade and hospitals. Everyone uses public services, so it's very important that we respect them and pay our taxes.

The **police** protect people, fight crime, enforce laws and control traffic.

The **fire brigade** helps when there is a fire, a flood or when someone is trapped.

The **health service** looks after people who are ill or need medical attention.

Education, such as schools and universities.

Health services, such as hospitals and health centres.

Public transport, such as buses and trains.

Social services help people in different ways, such as finding a home or a job. They also help elderly and disabled people.

④ Find out who the mayor of your town or city is. Where is the town or city hall located? Use the internet to help you.

⑤ Would you like to be a mayor? In groups, discuss why or why not. Think about responsibilities.

Road safety

Town and city councils also **manage the roads and traffic** so pedestrians and motorists can move around safely. The signs below are used to control traffic in Europe.

Road signs

Road signs have different shapes, colours and symbols. Some signs are for motorists and some are for pedestrians.

Signs with **red triangles** warn you about something ahead.

school ahead — slippery surface ahead

Signs with **red circles** tell you not to do something.

no parking — no cycling

A **pedestrian crossing** is a safe place to cross the road.

Signs that are **blue and round** tell you what you must do.

left turn — minimum speed 30 km/h

Signs that are **blue and rectangular** give you information.

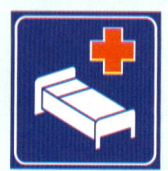 

hospital — cul-de-sac

Traffic lights help pedestrians and motorists move around safely.

1. Who manages the roads and traffic?
2. What do road signs with red triangles tell us? What about signs that are blue and round?
3. List five rules of the road.

Did you know?

Countries all around the world use this road sign.

The rules of the road

Everyone must respect road signs and know the rules of the road. These rules **keep everyone safe**. When walking around town, riding your bike or in the car, you must follow these rules:

Find a safe place to cross the road. Walk across the road – do not run!

Look and listen before you cross the road. Look to the left, then to the right and then to the left again.

Where there is no pavement, walk on the left-hand side of the road to face the traffic coming towards you.

Walk on the pavement, far from the kerb.

Always wear your seatbelt.

Always wear a helmet and the correct safety gear when riding a bike, skateboarding and roller-skating.

④ Why do we look left first before crossing the road?

⑤ Explain why it is important to walk and not run across the road.

⑥ On your way home from school, make a list of all the road signs you see. Count the pedestrian crossings too.

FIND OUT: Make a leaflet about where you live

Idea:

We can share information about our town or city with a leaflet.

- Paper
- Pen
- Photos
- Colouring materials
- Computer (optional)

Carry out:

Make a leaflet with information about interesting places in your town or city.

1 Find information about interesting places in your town or city. You can use the internet to help you.

2 Fold a sheet of paper in three. Design a cover for your leaflet and choose three places, one for each page.

3 Stick a photo or draw a picture on each page. Write information or print it out and stick it on.

Follow up:

1 Which places did you choose? Why?

2 Draw a map on the back of your leaflet to show where the places are located.

3 Are there any places in other towns that you would like to visit? Have you visited any places you really liked?

THINK ABOUT IT: Celebrating community

In the African Savannah of Kenya and Tanzania, groups of people called the Masai live in small communities. The men of the tribe are called warriors. Their main responsibility is to protect their cattle from lions. The community celebrates many ceremonies as the young boys grow up and become warriors. During these celebrations, the men participate in Adumu, which means the jumping dance. They sing and dance in a circle while each one takes turns to see who can jump the highest.

Some communities in India celebrate with their family and neighbours in a very colourful way. During the festival of Holi, all the members of the community, young and old, throw colourful powder at each other. Some people spray coloured water too. The neighbourhood children collect wood and the whole community helps to build a big fire. The people sing and dance in the streets to celebrate the beginning of spring together.

① What local festivals do you celebrate in your community?

② Why are festivals important?

③ In groups, make a poster about the festivals in your community. Write about the activities that are part of the festival. Add photos and draw pictures.

LOOK BACK: Community

Study skills

1 Copy and complete.

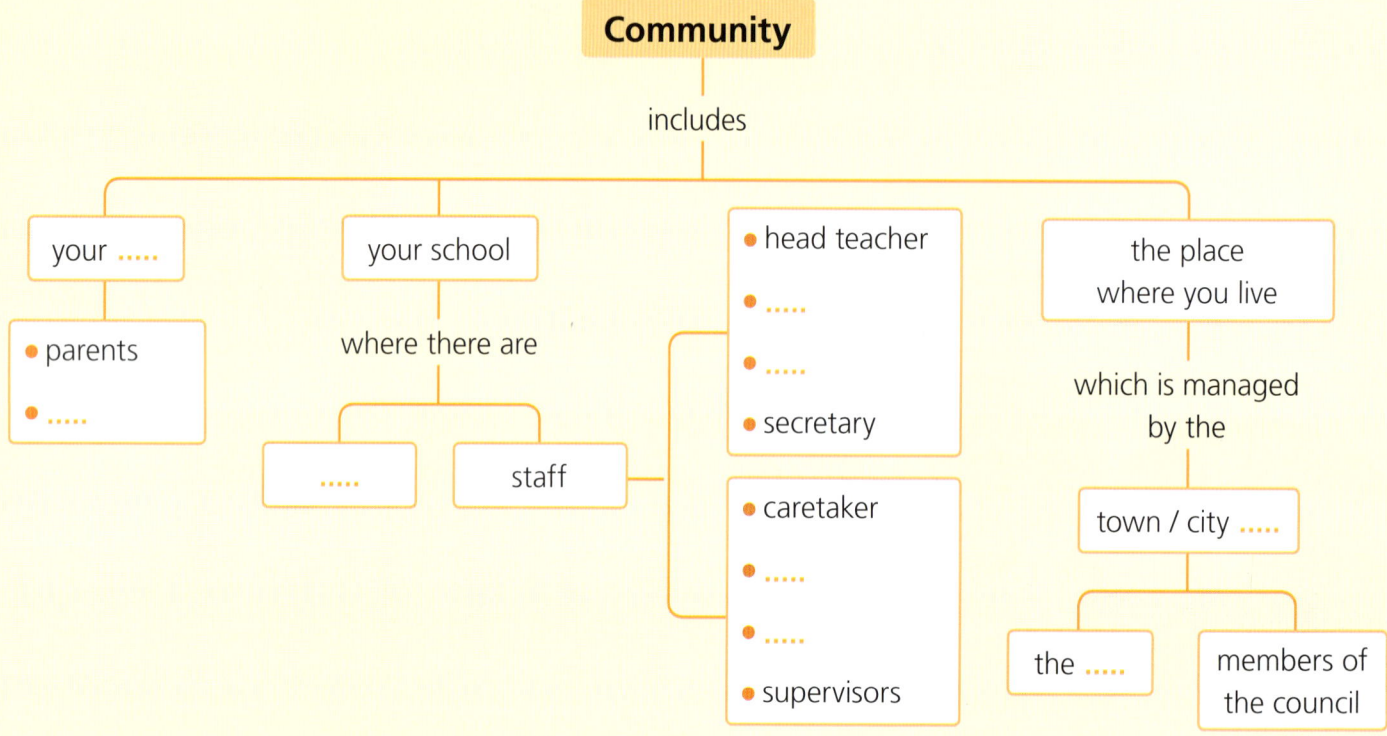

2 In pairs, use sticky notes to revise the unit.

- With your partner, open the book on page 24. Read the page.
- Write the page number and a title at the top of a sticky note.
- Then, write some words that help you to summarise the page and stick the note on the page.
- Do this for all pages up to page 29.
- When you finish, stick all the notes on the board. Put the notes for each page together to help you compare. For example, all the notes for page 29 go together.

Review

1 Match and write the sentences about the staff of a school.

1. The head teacher
2. The deputy head teacher
3. The teachers
4. The caretaker
5. The cooks
6. The supervisors

a. looks after the school buildings.
b. manages the school.
c. look after the pupils during break times.
d. prepare lunch and sometimes breakfast too.
e. teach classes.
f. helps the head teacher to manage the school.

2 Copy and complete the sentences.

> mayor   town council   police officer   fire brigade

a. The ..... is the head of the city council.

b. A ..... fights crime and controls traffic.

c. The ..... helps when there is a fire or a flood.

d. The ..... works in the town hall.

3 With your partner, discuss what each of these signs means.

A  B  C  D  E

4 Work in pairs. Play the true or false game.

Pupil A

a. All families are the same.
b. There are local elections every six years.
c. Road signs with red triangles tell you what you must do.

Pupil B

a. Pupils work at a school.
b. Public services are not for everyone.
c. Where there is no pavement, you should walk on the right-hand side of the road.

33

3 Where we live

A trip to the city centre

1 🔊 Listen and read.

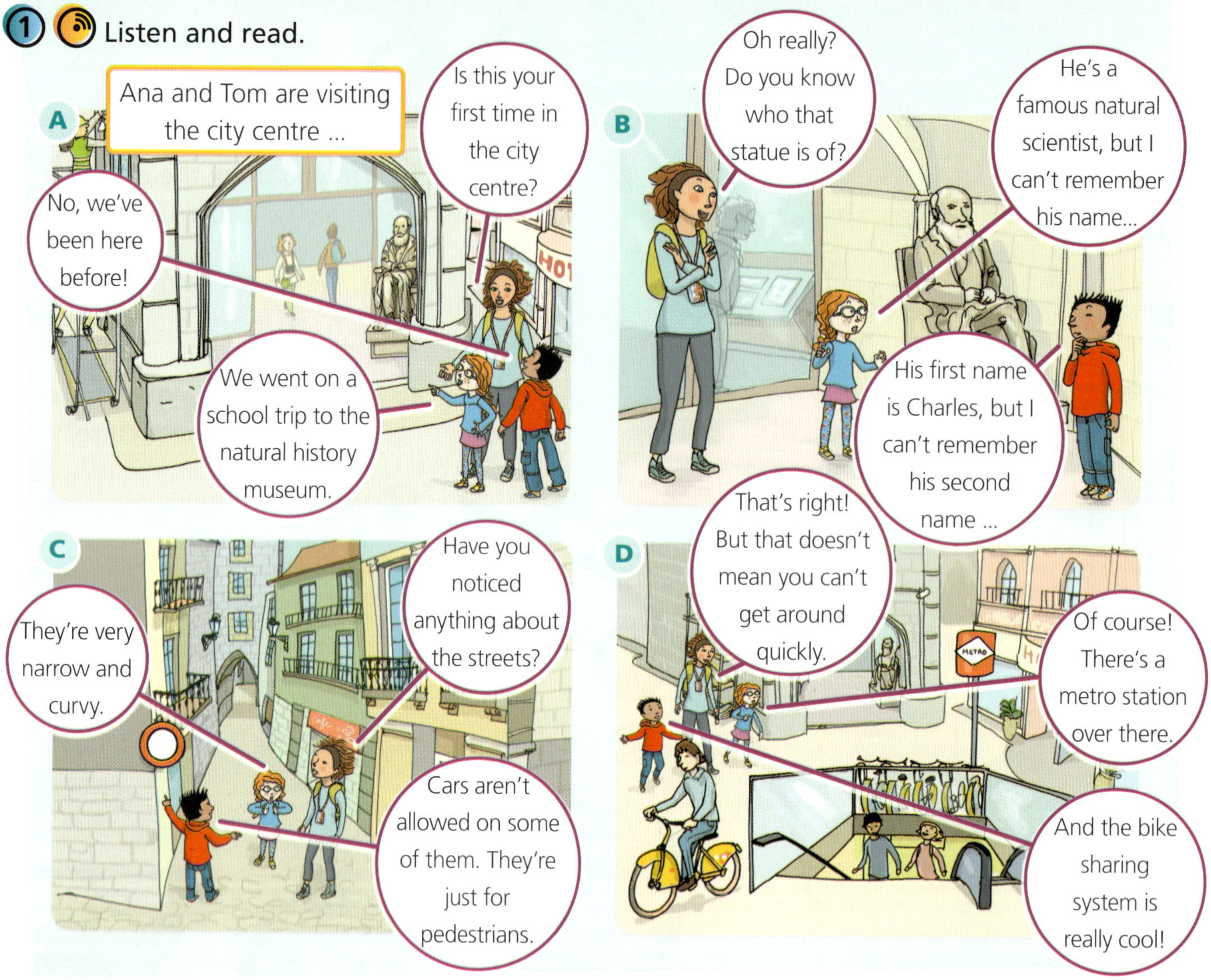

A Ana and Tom are visiting the city centre…
- Is this your first time in the city centre?
- No, we've been here before!
- We went on a school trip to the natural history museum.

B Oh really? Do you know who that statue is of?
- He's a famous natural scientist, but I can't remember his name…
- His first name is Charles, but I can't remember his second name…

C Have you noticed anything about the streets?
- They're very narrow and curvy.
- Cars aren't allowed on some of them. They're just for pedestrians.

D That's right! But that doesn't mean you can't get around quickly.
- Of course! There's a metro station over there.
- And the bike sharing system is really cool!

2 📖 Read the descriptions below and match them to the pictures.

1. We use this public service to get from one place to another.
2. We visit these places to learn about history, science and art.
3. We build these structures to celebrate or remember a person or an event, for example, a statue.
4. This is an open space in a city or town where we can go for a walk, for a picnic or to play.
5. This is a place where tourists and travellers pay to stay in a room and sometimes have meals.

36

Ana and Tom's school trip project

Look at Ana and Tom's project, then answer the questions.

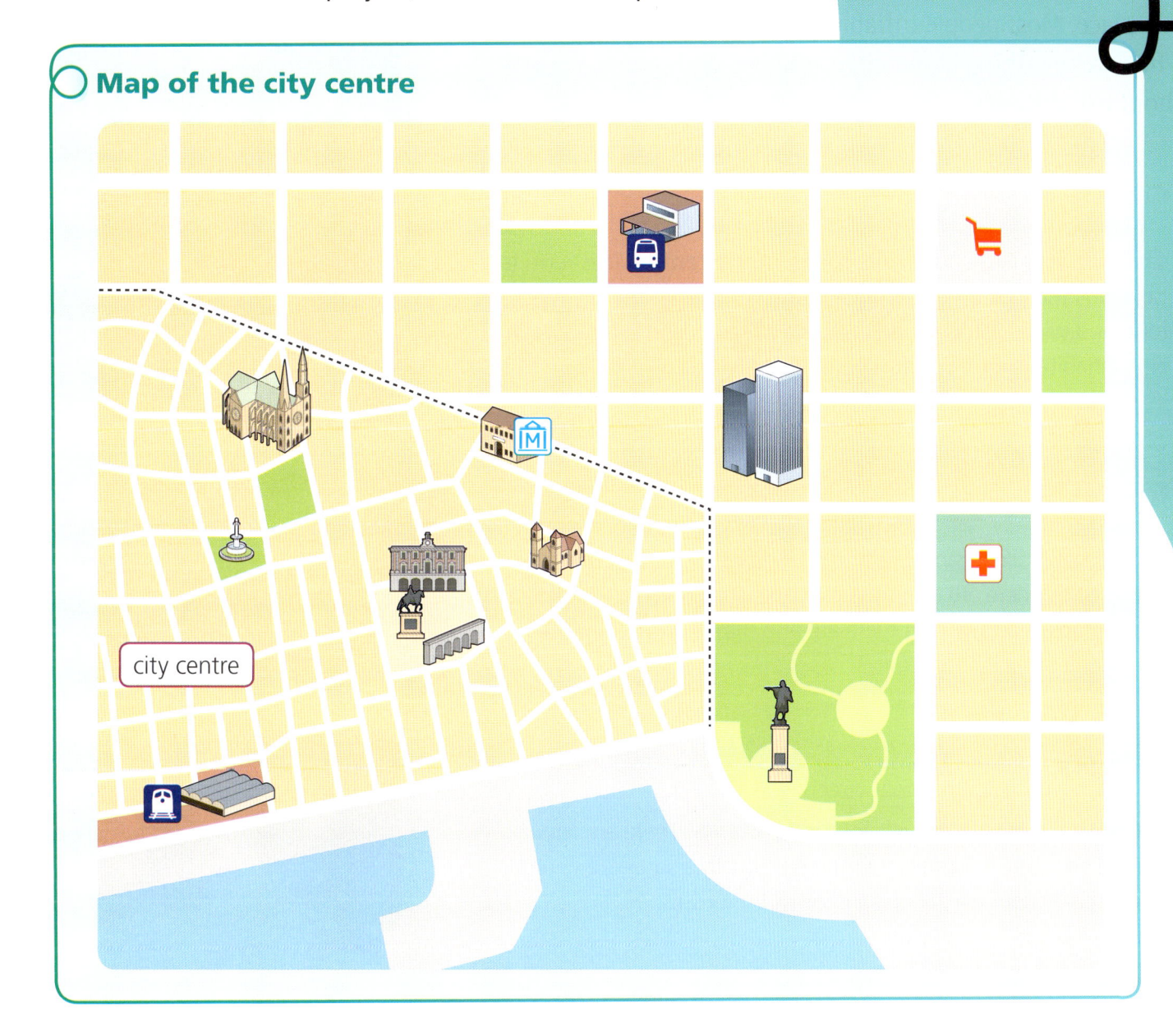

Map of the city centre

city centre

① Look at the map of the city. Find: the main square, a museum, a religious building, two monuments and a skyscraper.

② Look at the map. Compare the streets in the city centre to the streets outside. Are they different? Explain.

③ Find a tourist map of Rio de Janeiro or use Google Maps. Which is the oldest area? Explain your ideas.

We live in different places

Cities, towns and villages

We all **inhabit** a place – this is another way of saying we all live in a place. Most people inhabit cities, villages and towns. So, when we're talking about cities, villages and towns, we talk about **inhabitants**.

Cities

Cities are very large areas with **many inhabitants**. Cities have tall buildings that are used as homes or offices. Many of the streets are long and wide. You can find a variety of shops and businesses in a city. Inhabitants of cities also have access to **many public services**.

Towns

Towns are smaller than cities and have **fewer inhabitants**. Like in cities, there are also squares, parks and churches. You can find many shops in a town and there are also **many public services**.

Villages

Villages are small places with **few inhabitants**. There are **few public services** in villages, but there is usually a square, a church and a main street with shops and other businesses.

---

① Compare and contrast a city and a village. Think about size, inhabitants, shops and public services.

A city has ..... , but a village has ..... .

② Compare and contrast rural and urban areas. Think about space, public services, transport and jobs.

In urban areas there are ..... , but in rural areas there are ..... .

In other words

A very tall building with many floors is called a *skyscraper*. They are found in cities.

Urban and rural areas

Life in a big city is very different to life in a small village. Let's look at how urban and rural areas are different.

Urban areas

Cities and **large towns** are urban areas. Buildings are often close together, so there are few open spaces.

In urban areas there is a **large variety of public services**. Public transport, such as buses, trains and metro systems, help people get around.

In urban areas, there is a **large variety of jobs**. Some people work in shops; others work in big international companies.

Rural areas

Villages and some **small towns** are located in rural areas. Buildings are often far apart from each other, so there are more open spaces.

In rural areas, people often **share public services**, such as hospitals or schools, with other villages. Public transport is usually limited to buses.

There is **less variety of jobs** in rural areas. Some people work in shops; others in farming, fishing and mining.

③ Why are there more public services in urban areas than in rural areas?

④ Why do many people move from villages to cities? Discuss with a partner.

⑤ Find out which are the five largest cities in your country. What are their populations? You can use the internet to help you.

39

Areas of a city

Cities are constantly growing and changing. New **neighbourhoods** are being built all the time and they are often very different to the old ones.

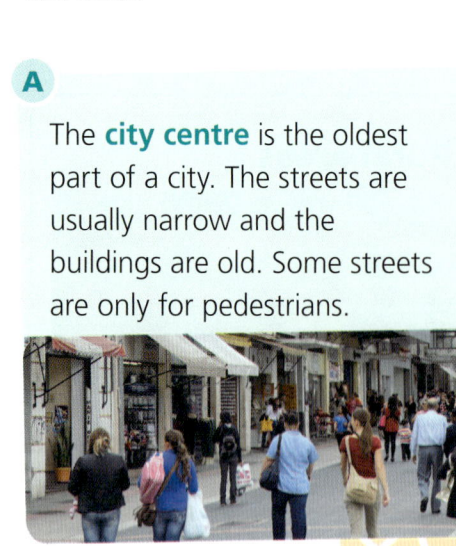

A

The **city centre** is the oldest part of a city. The streets are usually narrow and the buildings are old. Some streets are only for pedestrians.

The main square, city hall, churches and many monuments are found in the city centre.

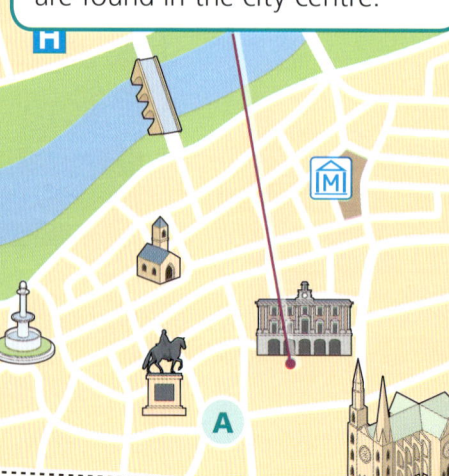

There is usually a train station near the city centre too.

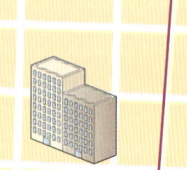

B

As the number of people living in the city centre grows, new, **modern neighbourhoods** are built.

There are usually lots of homes, offices and shops in modern neighbourhoods.

Modern neighbourhoods have wide, straight streets and the buildings are new.

① What can you find in the city centre?

② In which area of the city do we normally find these things?

- a. factory
- b. main square
- c. narrow streets
- d. wide streets
- e. airport
- f. city hall

③ How is taking the metro different from taking a bus?

In other words

In different countries, the metro has different names, such as the subway, the tube and the underground.

40

C

On the **outskirts** of the city, there is usually a lot of space to build new buildings for homes, offices and shops.

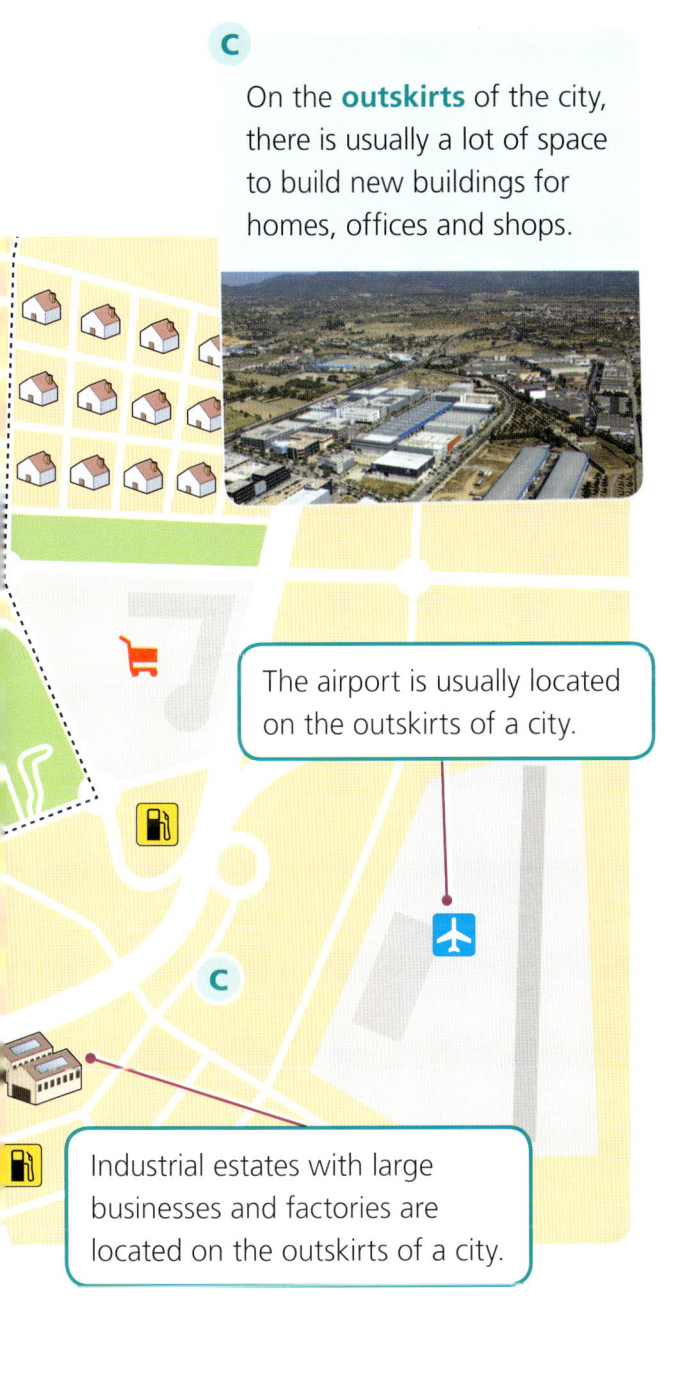

The airport is usually located on the outskirts of a city.

Industrial estates with large businesses and factories are located on the outskirts of a city.

Metro systems

Many large cities have a metro system that is mostly **underground**. It allows people to get from one area of a city to another quickly.

Look at this metro map. What is the quickest way to get from Waterloo Station to Liverpool Street Station?

Take the ..... line to ..... station and then take the ..... line to ..... station.

4) Choose two metro stations on different lines on the map and find the shortest route between them.

5) Investigate a city near where you live. How many people live there? What are the different areas of the city? What important monuments and buildings can you see there?

FIND OUT: How to make a bar chart

Idea:

We can show how many people do different things with a bar chart.

- Paper
- Pen
- Notebook
- Ruler
- Pencil
- Colouring materials

Carry out:

Do a class survey and show your results in a bar chart.

1 Make a table with a question to ask your classmates. Choose three to six possible answers.

2 Draw a vertical line and a horizontal line. Write the answers at the bottom and numbers at the side.

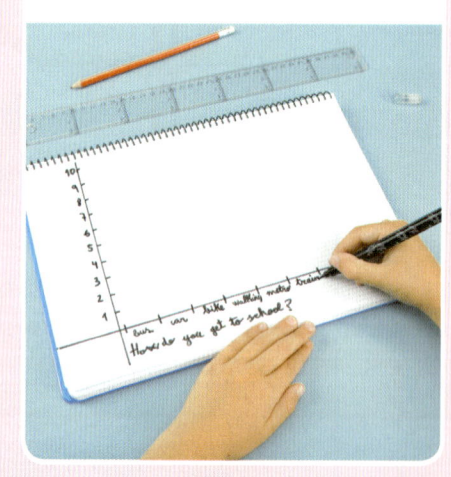

3 Ask your classmates the question. Record their answers. Draw and colour bars to show the data.

Follow up:

1. What is the most popular answer?

2. Which is the least popular?

3. What was the most surprising thing about your results?

4. What else could you show on a bar chart? Think of a question and possible answers.

42

THINK ABOUT IT: Protect your local monuments

Every town has important monuments. A monument is a structure that celebrates a person or a special event. They can teach us about history and our local culture. It is important to respect and protect our local monuments.

Look at these important monuments from all over the world. Do you know where each one is located?

A
B
C
D

Read this article about a community that wants to protect their local monuments.

LOCAL CITIZENS TAKE BACK ROME

In recent years, many of Rome's most historical monuments have been damaged by tourism, pollution and vandalism. Statues and monuments have been broken and ancient buildings have been covered in graffiti.

Some citizens are upset about this and they want to take action. They believe that the entire city of Rome is a museum and that all its monuments must be protected. Some of these citizens have formed an action group to try and solve a part of the problem. They meet up in their free time to clean the walls and paint over the graffiti. Now, they want their local government to help too.

1. Name some important monuments in your country.

2. Are there any important monuments where you live?

3. In groups, choose a monument. Use ICTs to make a presentation about why this monument is important.

LOOK BACK: Where we live

Study skills

1 Copy and complete.

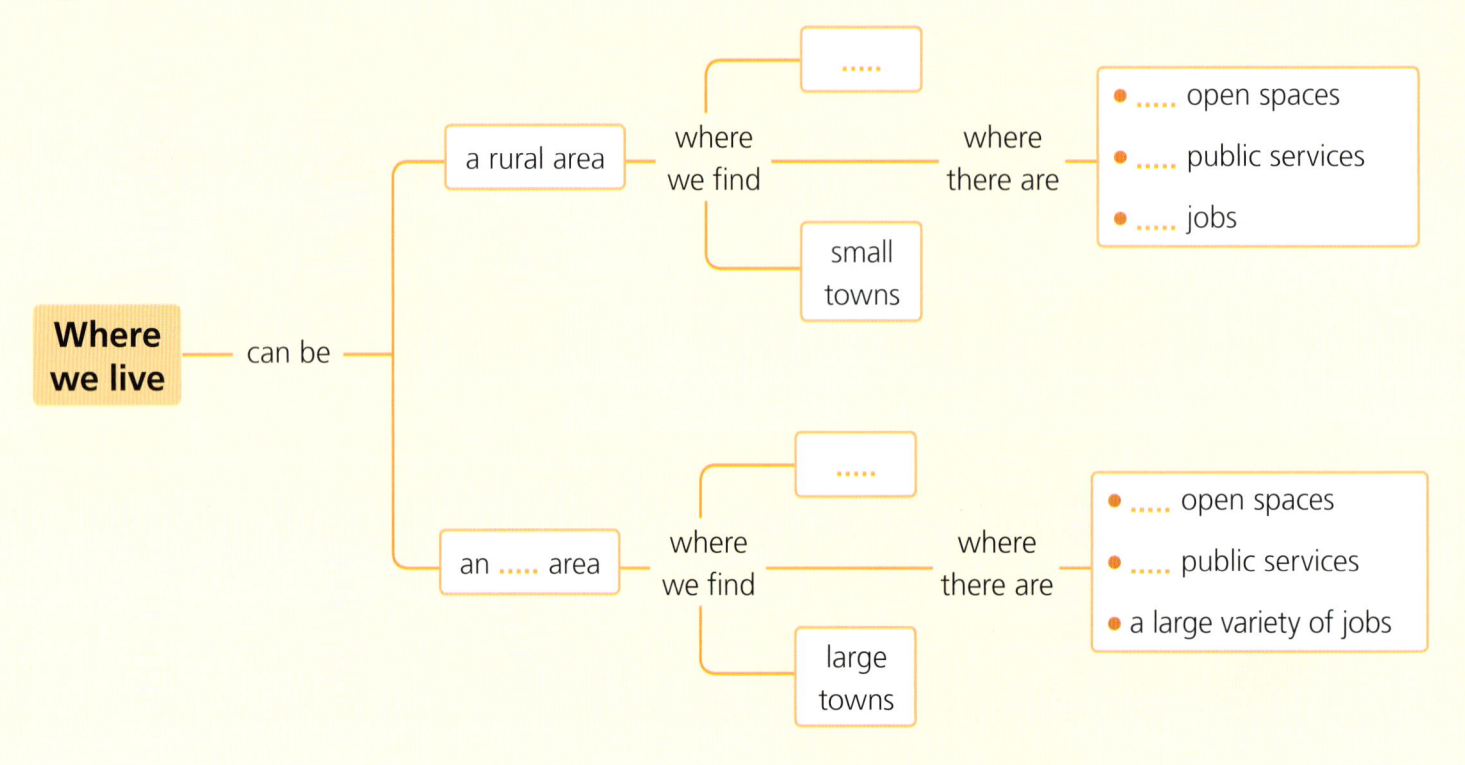

```
Where we live — can be
    ├── a rural area — where we find
    │       ├── .....
    │       └── small towns
    │           where there are
    │               • ..... open spaces
    │               • ..... public services
    │               • ..... jobs
    │
    └── an ..... area — where we find
            ├── .....
            └── large towns
                where there are
                    • ..... open spaces
                    • ..... public services
                    • a large variety of jobs
```

2 Use maps on the internet.

- Open an internet browser and type **maps.google.es** into the address bar.
- Type the name of a country, city, town or an address into the search bar.
- Use the + and − buttons to zoom in and zoom out.
- You can also choose a satellite view of the area.
- Drag the yellow man icon onto the map to get a view from the street.

Look at maps of other places you have visited or places you would like to visit.

Review

1 Copy and correct the sentences.

   a. A city has fewer inhabitants than a village.

   b. A village has more public services than a city.

   c. Cities are found in rural areas.

   d. There are more open spaces in urban areas.

2 Copy and match the areas of a city to the descriptions.

   a. The oldest part of the city.

   b. This area was built when the number of inhabitants in the city centre grew.

   c. There is a lot of space to build new buildings and factories in this area of the city.

   1. outskirts

   2. city centre

   3. modern neighbourhoods

3 Where do you find these things in a city?

A   B   C   D   E

4 Work in pairs. Use the words to ask each other questions.

Is there / Are there

- few
- many
- a small variety of
- a large variety of

- public services
- businesses
- open spaces
- offices
- inhabitants
- shops

in

- towns?
- villages?
- cities?
- rural areas?
- urban areas?

45

4 Time and history

46

Everything we do can be measured in time. It takes a certain amount of time to get out of bed in the morning, to get to school and to do our homework. History is also measured in time. It is the study of the past. It is important to learn about the past because it can help us to make the future better.

1. Find three old objects in the picture.

2. Find an example of art in the picture.

3. Which object do you think is the oldest in the picture?

4. Who is not behaving properly in the picture?

5. Listen to the song. Point to the words you hear.

axe

cave painting

history museum

pottery

fire

spear

A trip to the history museum

1 Listen and read.

A Ana and Tom are in the Prehistory room …

Wow! Ana, come and look at these clothes!

They must be thousands of years old.

B Actually, they're only five years old.

They're a replica of prehistoric clothes.

What? But they look so old!

C Why don't you have real prehistoric clothes in the museum?

Only fragments survive. The material breaks down over time and disappears.

D So, how do you know what the clothes looked like?

We looked at cave paintings from that time. They gave us some good ideas!

2 What is the museum tour guide describing? Listen and write it in your notebook.

A

B

C

D

48

Ana and Tom's school trip project

Look at Ana and Tom's project, then answer the questions.

Old and modern objects table

Old object	Modern object
(gramophone)	(mp3 player with earphones)
(candlestick telephone)	
(typewriter)	

1. Look at the old objects in the left-hand column. Draw or find photos of their modern equivalents in your notebook.

2. Make your own chart in your notebook. Find photos of old objects and their modern equivalents.

3. Think about what the objects you have chosen will look like in the future. Draw pictures in your notebook and label them.

Time and history

Past, present and future

Time is constantly moving forward. It never stops. We can talk about time in the **past**, **present** or **future**.

⬅ When we talk about the **past**, we talk about events that have already happened. Events in the past may have happened a long time ago or just yesterday.

⬇ The **present** includes events that are happening now, at this moment in time.

➡ When we talk about the **future**, we talk about events that have not happened yet. Events in the future can happen in 10 years' time or in five minutes' time.

Yesterday, two weeks ago, last year, in the past…

Tomorrow, next week, later, in the future…

Now, right now, at this moment, today…

History

History is the study of the past. People who study history are called **historians**. They study **historical sources** to find out information about the past.

Oral sources are things from the past that are told from person to person.

Physical sources are objects that give us information about the past. These objects can be as big as a castle or as small as a simple tool.

Written sources include books, letters, newspapers and other written documents from the past.

Visual sources can be paintings, drawings or photographs that show life in the past.

① What is history? What do historians do?

② Name four types of historical sources. Give an example of each one.

③ When will you be a decade old?

50

Measuring time

The history of human beings is very long. We use different **measurements of time** to organise information about the past.

There are 12 months in a **year**.

There are 10 years in a **decade**.

There are 100 years in a **century**.

There are 1 000 years in a **millennium**.

Things we use to measure time

We use different things to help us measure time in the past, present and future.

We use **watches** and **clocks** to measure time in hours, minutes and seconds.

Calendars help us measure time in days, weeks and months.

We use a **timeline** to show important events in the order they happened. They usually show us what happened during centuries or even millenniums. We can divide the past into five main periods of history:

Prehistory   Ancient History   The Middle Ages   The Early Modern Age   The Modern Age

4. Find out what an hourglass is. How does it work?

5. Make a timeline of your life. Include important events, such as when you were born, birthdays and special events.

6. Work with a group to make a timeline of your school year. Include when the school year started and important events, such as holidays and school trips.

51

Periods of history 1

Prehistory

Prehistory is the period from when the **first humans existed**, about two million years ago, to when **written history began**. The people who lived during this period didn't know how to write, but they left historical sources called **artefacts**. There were **two main periods** in Prehistory: the **Palaeolithic period** and the **Neolithic period**.

In the **Palaeolithic period**, people were nomads. This means that they moved from place to place to look for food and shelter. They used stone, wood and bones to make simple tools.

In the **Neolithic period**, people started to live in one place and form communities. They started to grow crops and keep domestic animals. They used stone and metal to make more complex tools.

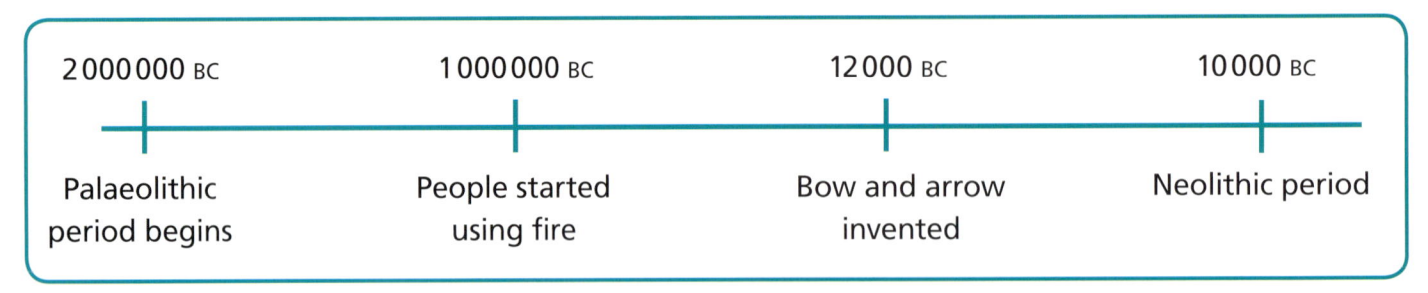

2 000 000 BC	1 000 000 BC	12 000 BC	10 000 BC
Palaeolithic period begins	People started using fire	Bow and arrow invented	Neolithic period

1. Identify the main differences between the Palaeolithic and Neolithic periods. Draw pictures to illustrate your ideas.

2. What historical sources give us information about the first humans?

3. Investigate prehistoric artefacts that have been found in your country.

52

Ancient History

Ancient History is the period from when **written history began** to the **fall of the Roman Empire**. During this time, great civilisations developed in countries such as Greece, Egypt, China and Mexico.

Each civilisation developed a different way of **writing**. For example Ancient Egyptians used **hieroglyphics** and the Romans wrote in **Latin**.

Latin

Egyptian hieroglyphics

Greek temple in Athens

Villa in Rome

People began to live in big **towns** and **cities**, such as Rome and Athens. They also built public and private **buildings**.

Ancient rice fields in China

They formed **governments**, wrote **laws**, developed skills and had **jobs**. They also made important advances in **agriculture**.

The letters SPQR refer to the Roman government.

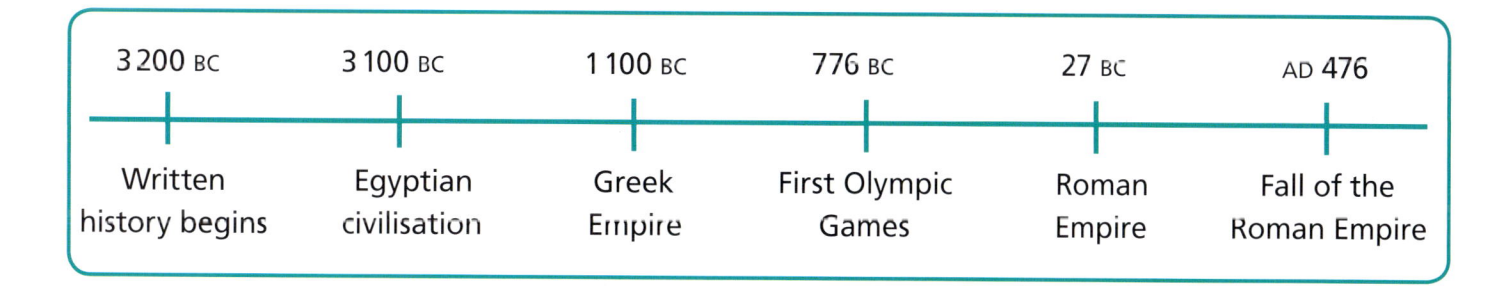

3 200 BC	3 100 BC	1 100 BC	776 BC	27 BC	AD 476
Written history begins	Egyptian civilisation	Greek Empire	First Olympic Games	Roman Empire	Fall of the Roman Empire

1. List three things that people in ancient civilisations did.

2. Choose a Roman structure in Europe. Find out what it was used for.

Periods of history 2

The Middle Ages

The Middle Ages began **about 1500 years ago**. During this period, the **Christian** and **Islamic** cultures were prominent in some areas of Europe. These areas were divided into **kingdoms**, usually ruled by a king.

In other words

The Middle Ages are also called Medieval Times or the Dark Ages in Europe.

People built **castles** and **walls** to defend their territory.

In Christian areas, **churches** and cathedrals were built.

In Islamic areas, **mosques** were built.

The Early Modern Age

The Early Modern Age began about five hundred years ago. Small kingdoms came together to form big countries with one king.

Explorers discovered new lands and products.

There were **discoveries** in **science**, such as electricity.

The invention of the **printing press** made it quicker and easier to produce books.

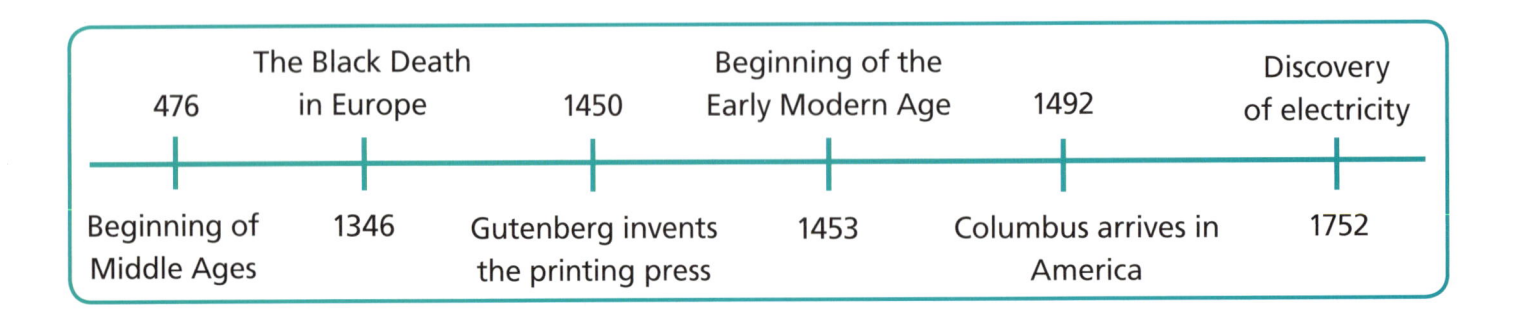

476		The Black Death in Europe		1450		Beginning of the Early Modern Age		1492		Discovery of electricity
Beginning of Middle Ages	1346		Gutenberg invents the printing press		1453		Columbus arrives in America		1752	

54

The Modern Age

The Modern Age began **about 200 years ago**. It was a time of industry and changes in society. New **inventions**, such as the **steam engine**, changed the way people lived and worked.

Cities grew and changed, with new streets and buildings. Public services, such as schools, hospitals and transport, became common.

Factories made mass-produced products. People moved to towns and cities to work in these factories, so **urban populations increased**.

With the invention of the telephone, radio and television, **communication** became easier.

Advances in **medicine** included the X-ray and vaccinations.

1769	Modern Age	1876	Invention of the radio	1923	Present day
Invention of the steam engine	1789	Invention of the telephone	1899	Invention of the television	

1. What were some important cultures in Europe during the Middle Ages?

2. How was the Early Modern Age different from the Middle Ages?

3. How did factories affect urban populations in the Modern Age?

4. Investigate the steam engine. How did it influence transport and the production of goods?

FIND OUT: Timelines

Idea:
We can make a timeline to learn about the history of our local area.

- Card
- Paper
- Glue stick
- Pencil
- Photos
- Colouring materials
- Computer (optional)

Carry out:
Make a timeline of the history of your local area.

1 Find a photo of a place of historical interest in your local area or take a photo of it yourself.

2 Find out information about the place, for example, when it was built. Write a short description of it.

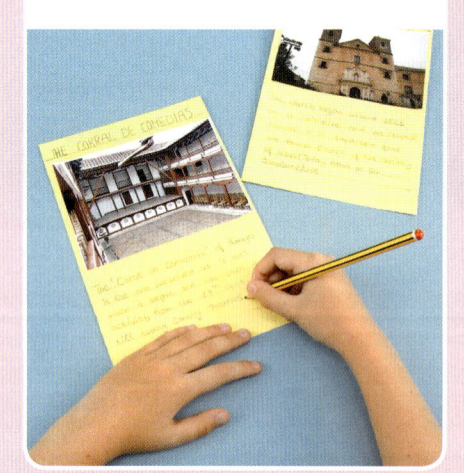

3 Put the places in order on a timeline, from past to present. Write periods, such as 17th Century.

Follow up:

1. Which historical sources did you use?

2. Which place of historical interest do you think is most interesting?

3. Describe how your local area has changed over time.

56

THINK ABOUT IT: Traditions from the past

Traditions are an important part of history. They are passed down from generation to generation. Many traditions from around the world include food, clothes, music, dance and crafts. Read about some different traditions and match them to the photos below.

1 Rice and noodles are traditional foods that Japanese people have eaten for thousands of years.

2 Traditional clothes in Peru are made from alpaca wool. People have worn the same bright colours for generations.

3 Sevillanas is a type of music and dance from Andalucía, Spain. It first appeared in the 15th Century and is still very popular today.

4 The bagpipes are a traditional musical instrument from Scotland. They are are also popular in other countries in Europe.

5 Pysanka is an ancient tradition of decorating eggs in Ukraine. Families continue to decorate eggs to celebrate spring.

① Can you think of any traditional celebrations that take place in your local area?

② In a group, investigate traditions in your country. Use ICTs to present information about traditional food, clothes, music, dance trand crafts.

LOOK BACK: Time and history

Study skills

1 Copy and complete.

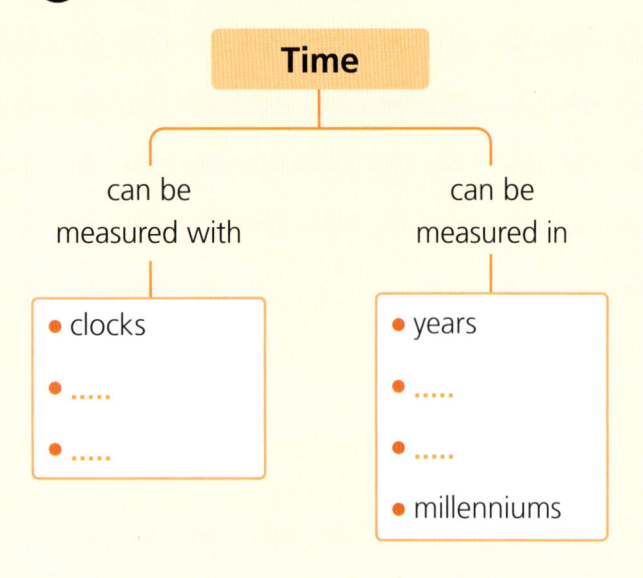

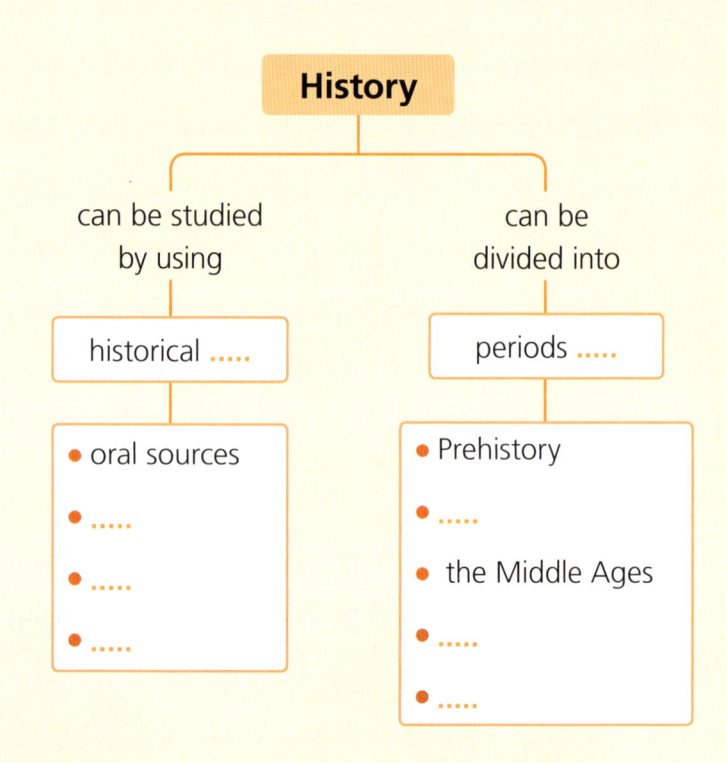

Time

can be measured with
- clocks
- .....
- .....

can be measured in
- years
- .....
- .....
- millenniums

History

can be studied by using
- historical .....
- oral sources
- .....
- .....
- .....

can be divided into
- periods .....
- Prehistory
- .....
- the Middle Ages
- .....
- .....

2 What type of learner are you?

Did you know we all learn in different ways? Read the descriptions below and decide which type of learner you are.

a. **Visual learners:** use words, illustrations and diagrams to revise. Memorise by writing.

b. **Physical learners:** learn by doing physical things and games. Memorise by using actions.

c. **Auditory learners:** learn by talking and listening. Memorise by repeating words.

Review

1 Copy and complete the table with the sentences.

a. People made simple tools.

b. People started to grow crops and keep domestic animals.

c. People formed communities.

d. People made more complex tools.

e. People were nomads.

Palaeolithic period	Neolithic period

2 Copy and complete the text about Ancient History.

Ancient History is the period from when written ..... began. Great ..... developed in countries such as Greece, Egypt, China and Mexico. They built cities and wrote ..... . Important advances were also made in ..... .

agriculture   history   civilisations   laws

3 Copy and match the sentences about the Middle Ages.

a. The Middle Ages .....

b. Many areas of Europe were .....

c. Most kingdoms .....

d. People built .....

..... castles and walls to defend their territory.

..... began about 1 500 years ago.

..... had a king.

..... divided into kingdoms.

4 Work in pairs. Order the questions and test your partner.

Pupil A

a. measure / things / we / use / to / what / do / time ?

b. did / the / begin / Modern / when / Age ?

c. was / steam / important / engine / an / why / invention / the ?

Pupil B

a. was / used / print / which / books / invention / to ?

b. discover / Columbus / did / Christopher / what ?

c. Age / the / when / begin / Modern / did ?

5 Matter, materials and mixtures

What is matter? Anything we can see, touch, taste or smell is matter. In other words, everything on our planet and in the Universe is made up of matter. Even you are made up of matter!

The words *matter* and *material* can be confusing. Materials are made up of matter, and we use materials to make things.

1. Identify a liquid, a solid and a gas in the picture.

2. Name some different materials you can see in the picture.

3. How many flexible materials can you see?

4. Which materials in the picture do you recycle?

5. Listen to the song. Copy the words you hear.

plastic

wood

glass

paper

metal

fabric

61

A trip to a recycling plant

1 🔊 Listen and read.

A Alex and Carla are looking at some recyclable materials ...

Hmmm ... We put liquids in them?

They're waterproof!

Can you tell me anything about these bottles? What are their properties?

B This one is smooth.

This one is too!

Any other properties?

C Can you change their shape?

My bottle is flexible. I can crush it!

Grrr! I can't. It's rigid.

D Can you break them?

I'm not going to try. Glass is fragile!

It's impossible. Plastic is resistant!

2 Look at the story. Write one or two words to complete the sentences.

1. Alex and Carla are on a school trip to a ..... .

2. A ..... is smooth and rigid, but it is also fragile.

3. A ..... is rough, rigid and resistant.

4. One side of a ..... is absorbant and the other side is rough.

5. A ..... is waterproof, flexible and smooth.

plastic bottle

glass bottle

kitchen sponge

recycling plant

wooden pallet

Alex and Carla's school trip project

Look at Alex and Carla's project, then answer the questions.

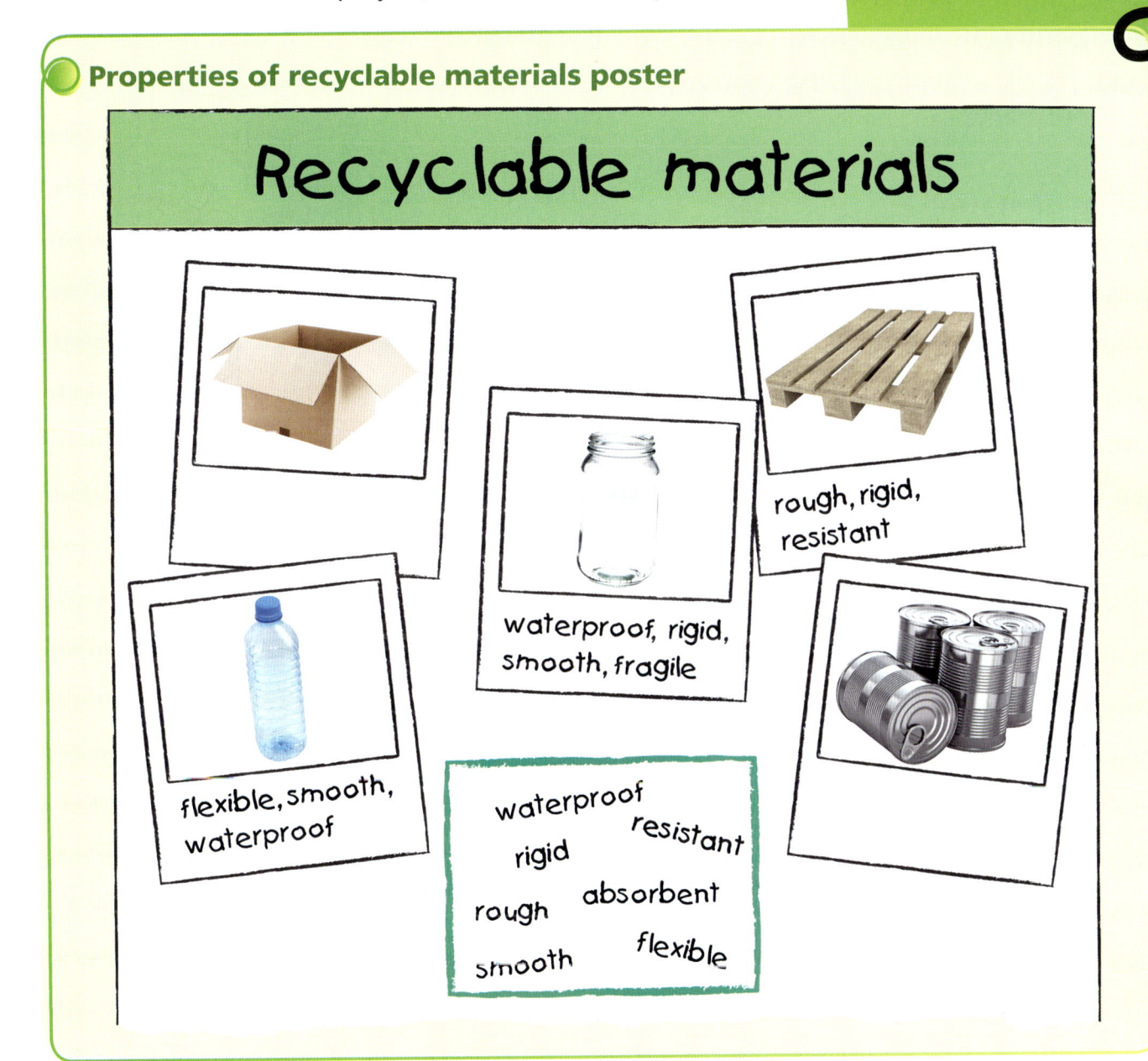

Properties of recyclable materials poster

Recyclable materials

- (cardboard box)
- (glass jar) waterproof, rigid, smooth, fragile
- (wooden pallet) rough, rigid, resistant
- (plastic bottle) flexible, smooth, waterproof
- (tin cans)

waterproof   resistant   rigid   rough   absorbent   smooth   flexible

1. Copy and complete the project in your notebook. Add two more objects and the words to describe them.

2. Carla wants to add the word *resistant* to some of the objects. Which objects?

3. All of these objects are made up of different materials (metal, plastic, wood, etc.). Where do we get them from?

Matter changes

Physical changes

Matter has different **properties**, like **shape**, **size** and **state**. These properties can change. These changes are called **physical changes**. Try the simple experiments below to see how the properties of matter can change.

Change of state

We can change the **state** of water from a **liquid** to a **solid** by freezing it and making ice. What happens when we heat it? Does it change state?

Change of shape

We can **bend**, **twist**, **press** and **stretch** plasticine. The plasticine **stays in the new shape** when we stop applying force. What happens to a rubber band when we stretch it? What happens when we let go?

---

1. Draw the three states of water. Write some examples of solid water, liquid water and water vapour.

2. Make a list of the things in your classroom whose shape you can change with force.

3. What reaction occurs when we burn paper? And when rust forms on metal?

Did you know?

Rubber bands last longer if we keep them in a container in the fridge. Why do you think this happens?

Chemical changes

Sometimes matter **reacts** with **air**, **water** and **other elements**. These reactions cause the matter to **change into different matter**. These reactions are called **chemical changes**.

Combustion

When we **burn** paper, there is a reaction called **combustion**. The paper changes into different matter and becomes **ash**. Do you think it is possible to change the ash back into paper?

Oxidation

If you leave your bike outside in the rain for a long time, the metal starts to turn **brown** and **rough**. This isn't dirt – it's called **rust**. The metal reacts with water and air (oxygen) and changes into different matter.

4 Test what happens to chocolate when you heat it and then leave it to cool. Compare and contrast this with what happens to ice.

5 Cut an apple in half and leave it for a while. What happens? What do you think the apple reacts with?

Mixtures

A **mixture** is something that contains **two or more different materials**. Almost everything around us is a mixture, including the air we breathe. In some mixtures we can see the different materials; in others it is impossible to see the different materials. Try making the mixtures below – some of them are delicious!

We can see the different materials.

Try making these mixtures!
- oil and vinegar
- chocolate chips and breadcrumbs
- soil and sand

Try making these mixtures!
- chocolate powder and milk
- sugar and butter
- detergent and water

We can't see the different materials.

① Describe the two types of mixtures in your own words.

② Put the following mixtures into two groups: sea water, muesli, milkshake, paint, fruit cake.

③ Which separation method do you think is best for separating sand and water? What about sand and pebbles?

④ Use drawings to explain the difference between filtering and sieving.

Separating materials in a mixture

Do you think it is possible to **separate** the different materials in a mixture? We can separate some materials in a mixture by **sieving**, **filtering** or **evaporating**. Follow the steps below and learn about these three methods.

Sieving: good for separating solids of different sizes

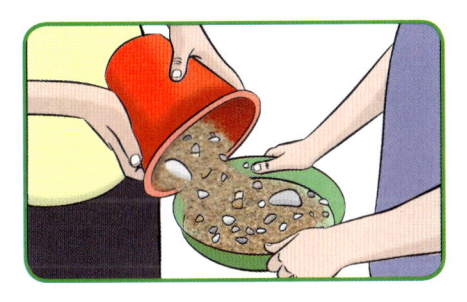

Filtering: good for separating solids and liquids

Evaporating: good for separating a solid that is dissolved in a liquid

⑤ What is the person in this photo doing? Explain why they are using this method of separation.

⑥ Predict what you would see if you evaporated a cup of black coffee. Test your idea.

67

Where do materials come from?

We can classify materials into **natural materials** and **manufactured materials**. Natural materials come from **living things** or from the **ground**. Manufactured materials are **processed** from natural materials or chemicals.

Natural materials

From plants

cotton

wood

From animals

feathers

wool

From the ground

slate

iron

crude oil

① Write a definition for *natural materials* and *manufactured materials*.

② What do we use wood, cotton and feathers for? Make a list.

Manufactured materials

We make paper from wood.

Trees are cut down.  → The wood is transported to a factory. 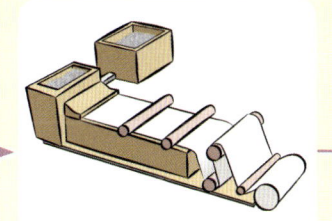 → The wood is processed into paper.  → Paper is used to make books and other products.

We make fabric from wool.

Sheep are sheared to obtain wool.  → The wool is transported to a factory. 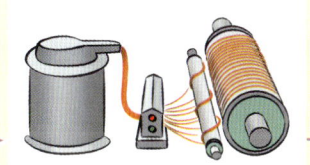 → The wool is processed into fabric.  → Fabric is used to make clothes and other products.

We make plastic from crude oil.

Crude oil is extracted from underground deposits. 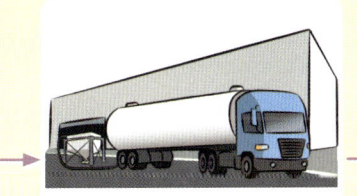 → The oil is transported to a factory. 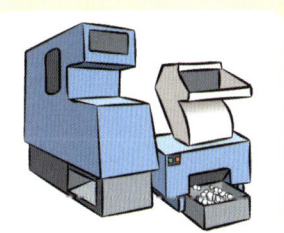 → The oil is refined and processed into plastic. → Plastic is used to make lots of different products.

(3) Investigate what other products are made from crude oil.

(4) A lot of waste is plastic. Did you know it can be recycled? Find out what we can make with recycled plastic.

FIND OUT: More about mixtures

Idea:
Sometimes we can't see the different materials in a mixture.

- Different materials
- Container of water
- Spoon

Test:
Mix different materials with water.

1 Half-fill a container with cold water.

2 Add one spoon of coffee. Stir and observe what happens.

3 Can you see the two different materials in the mixture?

Conclusions

1 You can repeat the procedure with these materials: soil, chocolate powder, bread, salt and olive oil.

2 In your notebook, create a chart to show your results. Use these headings:

We can see the different materials.

We can't see the different materials.

THINK ABOUT IT: Different materials, different uses

Have you ever thought about why umbrellas, raincoats and rubber boots protect us from the rain?

We use different materials because of their properties. Look at the objects in the pictures. Think about what they are made of and why we use these materials. Use the words to help.

absorbent • rough • soft • flexible

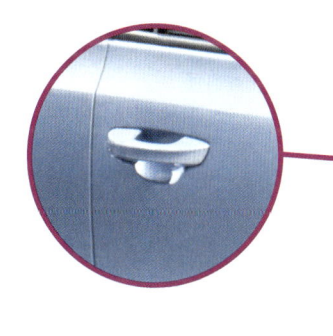

hot • protect • strong • melt

aluminium • rust • light • resistant

1. Choose five objects from school or from home. Think about what they are made of and why. You can use the internet to check your ideas.

2. Look at your shoes. How many different materials are they made of? Explain why each part is made of a different material.

LOOK BACK: Matter, materials and mixtures

Study skills

1 Copy and complete.

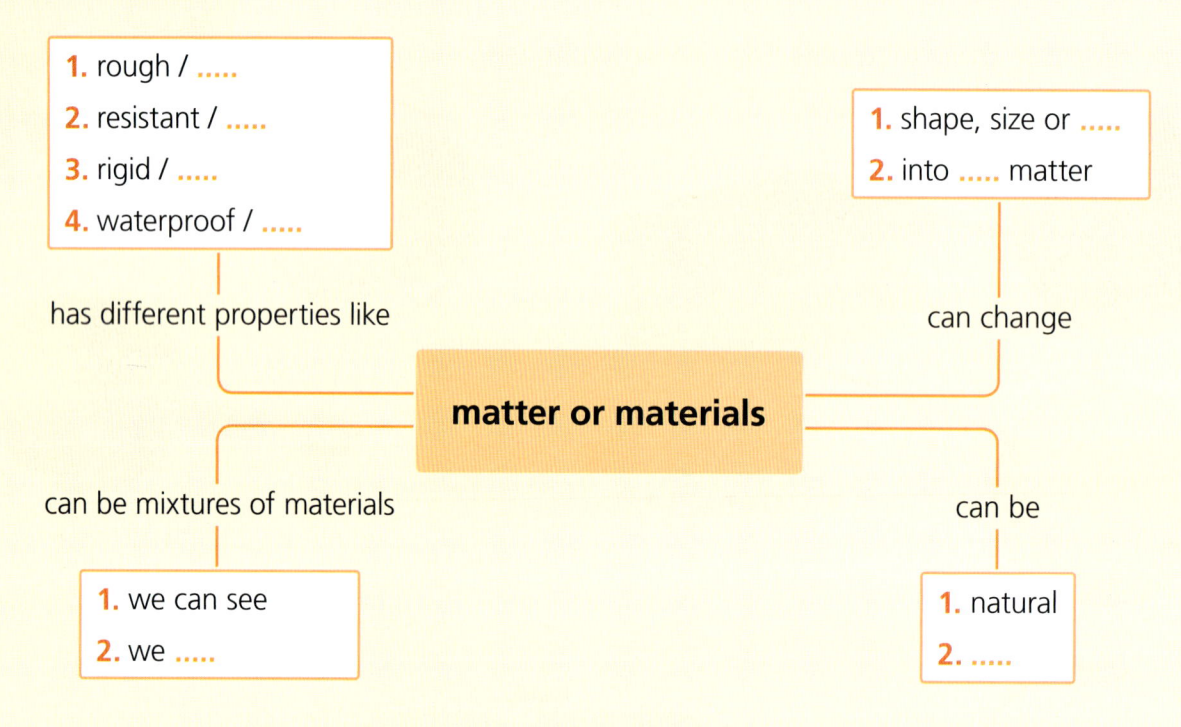

- 1. rough / .....
- 2. resistant / .....
- 3. rigid / .....
- 4. waterproof / .....

has different properties like

- 1. shape, size or .....
- 2. into ..... matter

can change

matter or materials

can be mixtures of materials

- 1. we can see
- 2. we .....

can be

- 1. natural
- 2. .....

2 Find images on the internet to help the whole class revise.

- Open a search engine and type in some key words from the unit, for example, *underground mining*.
- Click on *Images* at the top of the page. You will see lots of pictures.
- Click on a picture to make it bigger. Right-click on it and select *Copy Image*.
- Open a slideshow presentation document. Right-click and select *Paste*.
- Repeat steps 1–4 in new slides.
- Use the presentation to test your classmates. Can they remember the key words?

You can prepare a presentation for any unit in this book!

Review

1 Copy and complete the sentences.

a. Matter has three different ..... . It can be a gas, a liquid or a solid.

b. When water changes from a solid to a liquid, it is a ..... change.

c. Combustion and oxidation are ..... changes.

d. A mixture is something that contains different ..... .

e. Sieving, ... , and evaporating are methods of ..... materials in a mixture.

2 Look at the pictures. Describe what you see. Think about everything we have studied in this unit.

3 Work in pairs. Use the table to ask each other questions.

Is / Are	newspapers / plastic cups / wood / umbrellas / metal spoons / sand / bricks / rubber bands	flexible? / rigid? / resistant? / fragile? / smooth? / rough? / waterproof? / absorbent?

6 Energy

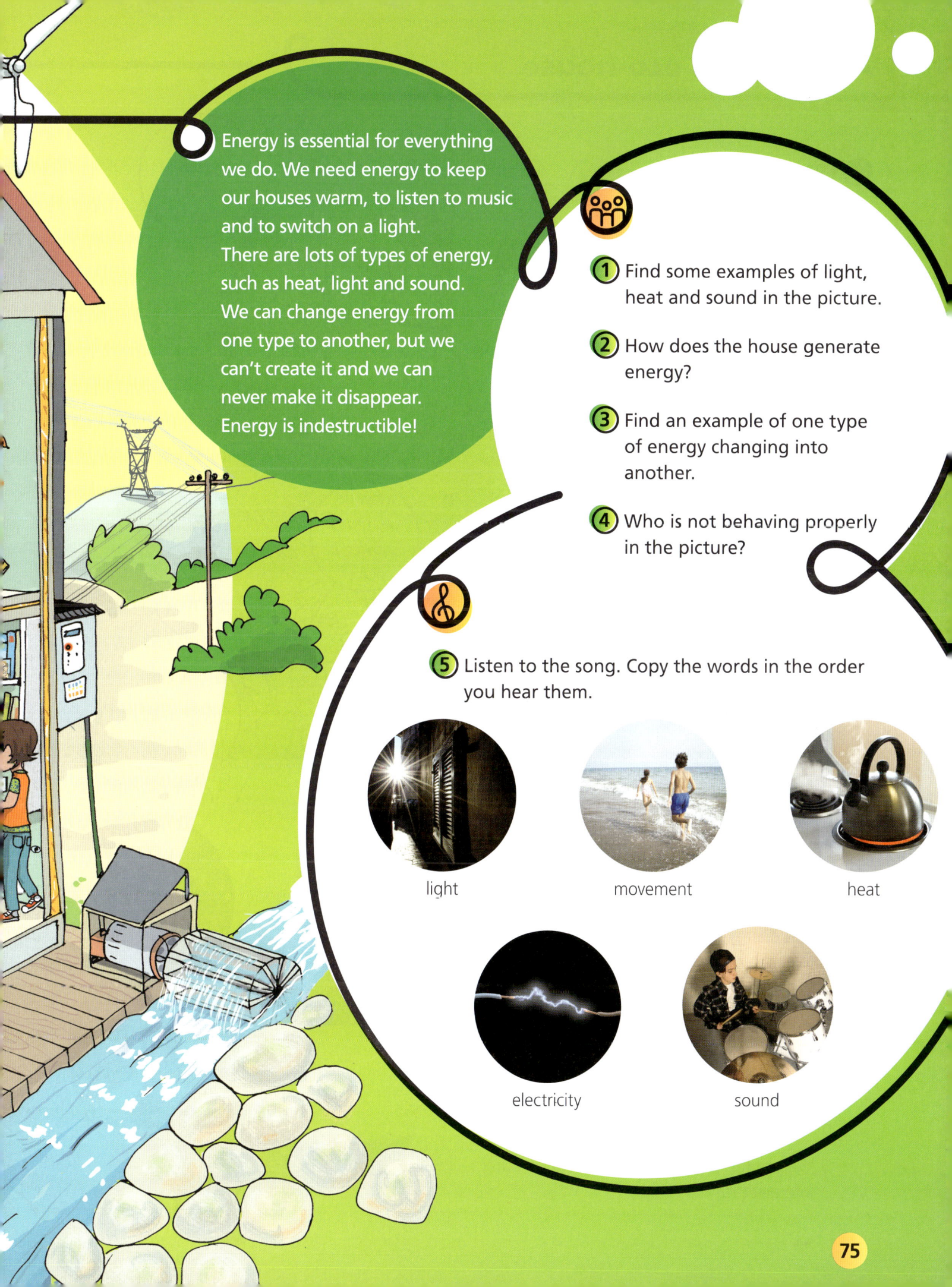

Energy is essential for everything we do. We need energy to keep our houses warm, to listen to music and to switch on a light. There are lots of types of energy, such as heat, light and sound. We can change energy from one type to another, but we can't create it and we can never make it disappear. Energy is indestructible!

1. Find some examples of light, heat and sound in the picture.

2. How does the house generate energy?

3. Find an example of one type of energy changing into another.

4. Who is not behaving properly in the picture?

5. Listen to the song. Copy the words in the order you hear them.

light

movement

heat

electricity

sound

A trip to an eco-house

1 🔊 **Listen and read.**

A Alex and Carla are learning about renewable energy …

Why is there a windmill on the roof of your house?

It's a wind turbine. It generates electricity for my house.

B What does this waterwheel do?

The water falls on it and moves the wheel. That generates electricity.

C Do these solar panels generate electricity?

No, I use them to heat water.

D How do you have a shower at night?

Sometimes I have to use non-renewable electricity.

2 🛡 **Read the descriptions and match them to the pictures.**

1. We use these to turn wind energy into electricity.

2. This energy source is a gas. We obtain it from the ground and use it for heat and for cooking.

3. This energy source is a solid. We obtain it from the ground and use it to produce heat.

4. We use these to turn solar energy into electricity or heat.

5. We use this to turn the movement of water into electricity.

Alex and Carla's school trip project

Look at Alex and Carla's project, then answer the questions.

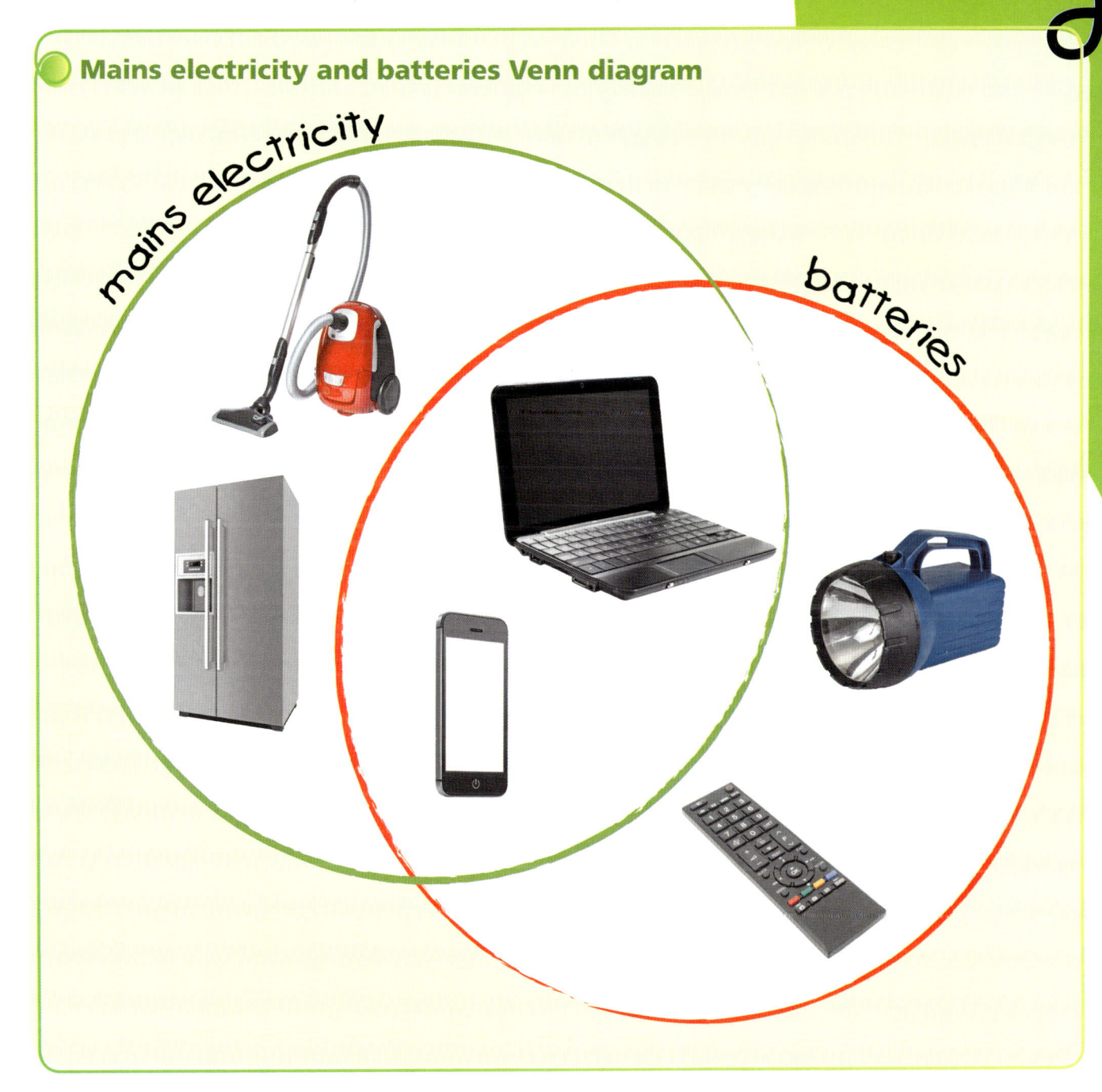

Mains electricity and batteries Venn diagram

1. Copy the chart in your notebook. Add four more devices.

2. Think of some advantages and disadvantages of using batteries.

3. What do you do with batteries when they are dead? Should you just throw them in the bin? Investigate.

Different types of energy

There are many different types of energy. We are going to look at the **six most important types**. Look at the picture and read about the different types of energy that we find all around us.

Thermal energy produces heat. The Sun produces lots of thermal energy and heats our planet. Find a man-made source of heat in the picture.

Moving things have **kinetic energy**. When we ride a bike we turn the chemical energy from the food we eat into kinetic energy. Look at the kite. What is making it move?

Food contains **chemical energy**. Our body turns this energy into thermal or kinetic energy. Find another example of chemical energy in the picture.

① Find five examples of sound and electrical energy in the picture. Write them in your notebook.

② Copy and complete the sentences.

   a. A car engine turns chemical energy into ..... energy.

   b. A radiator turns electrical energy into ..... energy.

   c. A radio turns electrical energy into ..... energy.

Link it up

When something burns (combustion), two types of energy are produced: thermal energy and light energy.

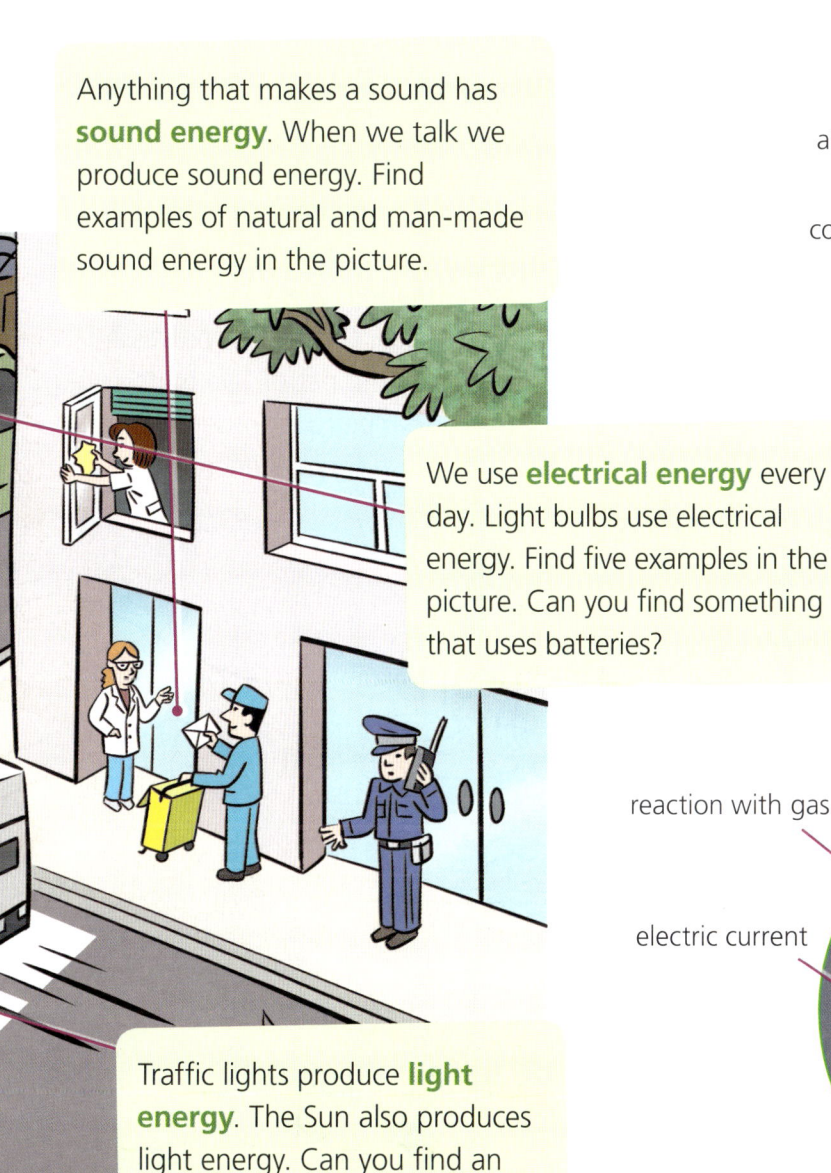

Anything that makes a sound has **sound energy**. When we talk we produce sound energy. Find examples of natural and man-made sound energy in the picture.

We use **electrical energy** every day. Light bulbs use electrical energy. Find five examples in the picture. Can you find something that uses batteries?

Traffic lights produce **light energy**. The Sun also produces light energy. Can you find an example of a living thing that needs light energy to live?

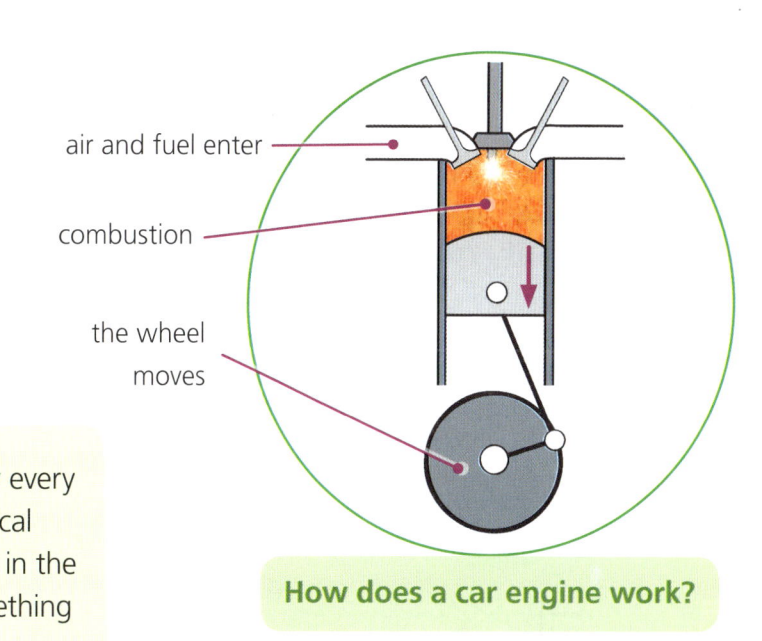

air and fuel enter

combustion

the wheel moves

How does a car engine work?

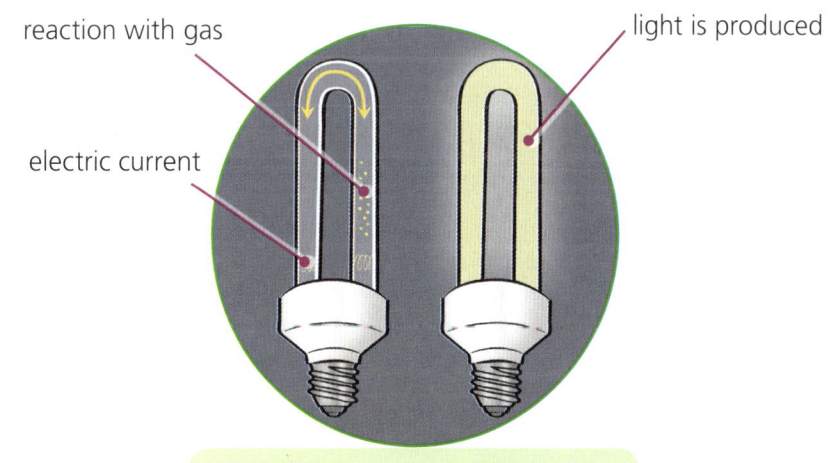

reaction with gas

light is produced

electric current

How does a light bulb work?

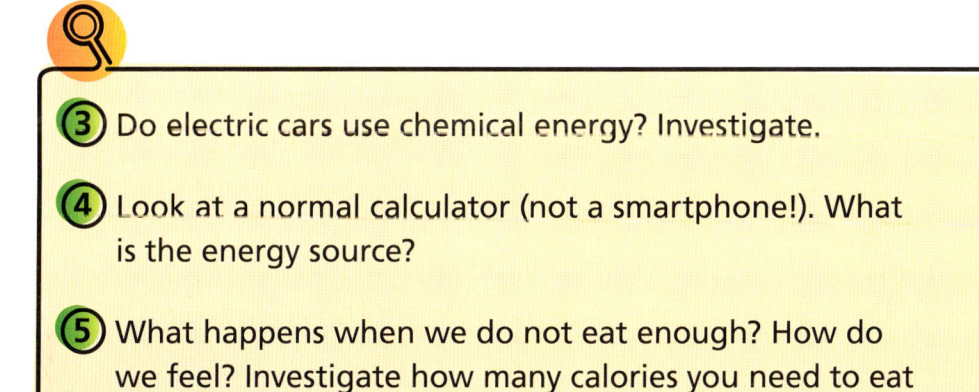

③ Do electric cars use chemical energy? Investigate.

④ Look at a normal calculator (not a smartphone!). What is the energy source?

⑤ What happens when we do not eat enough? How do we feel? Investigate how many calories you need to eat each day to get enough energy.

79

Sources of energy

Non-renewable energy

Non-renewable energy sources come **from the ground and the seabed**. We cannot replace these natural materials and they will eventually **run out**.

Crude oil comes from the ground or from the seabed. We extract it using **drills**. Crude oil is processed into petrol. We burn petrol to produce thermal energy.

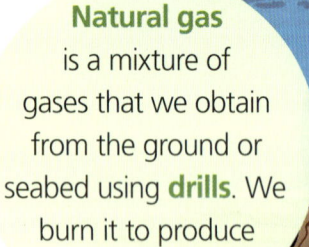

Natural gas is a mixture of gases that we obtain from the ground or seabed using **drills**. We burn it to produce thermal energy.

Coal comes from the ground. We **mine** it and burn it to produce thermal energy.

1. In your own words, write definitions for renewable and non-renewable energy.
2. Explain what solar panels and wind turbines do.
3. What do crude oil, coal and natural gas have in common? Compare and contrast.

In other words

Coal, oil and natural gas are called *fossil fuels* because they take millions of years to form.

80

Renewable energy

We can also use the **Sun**, **wind** and **water** as sources of energy. These are renewable sources of energy because they **do not run out**. They are much better for the environment because they **do not cause pollution**.

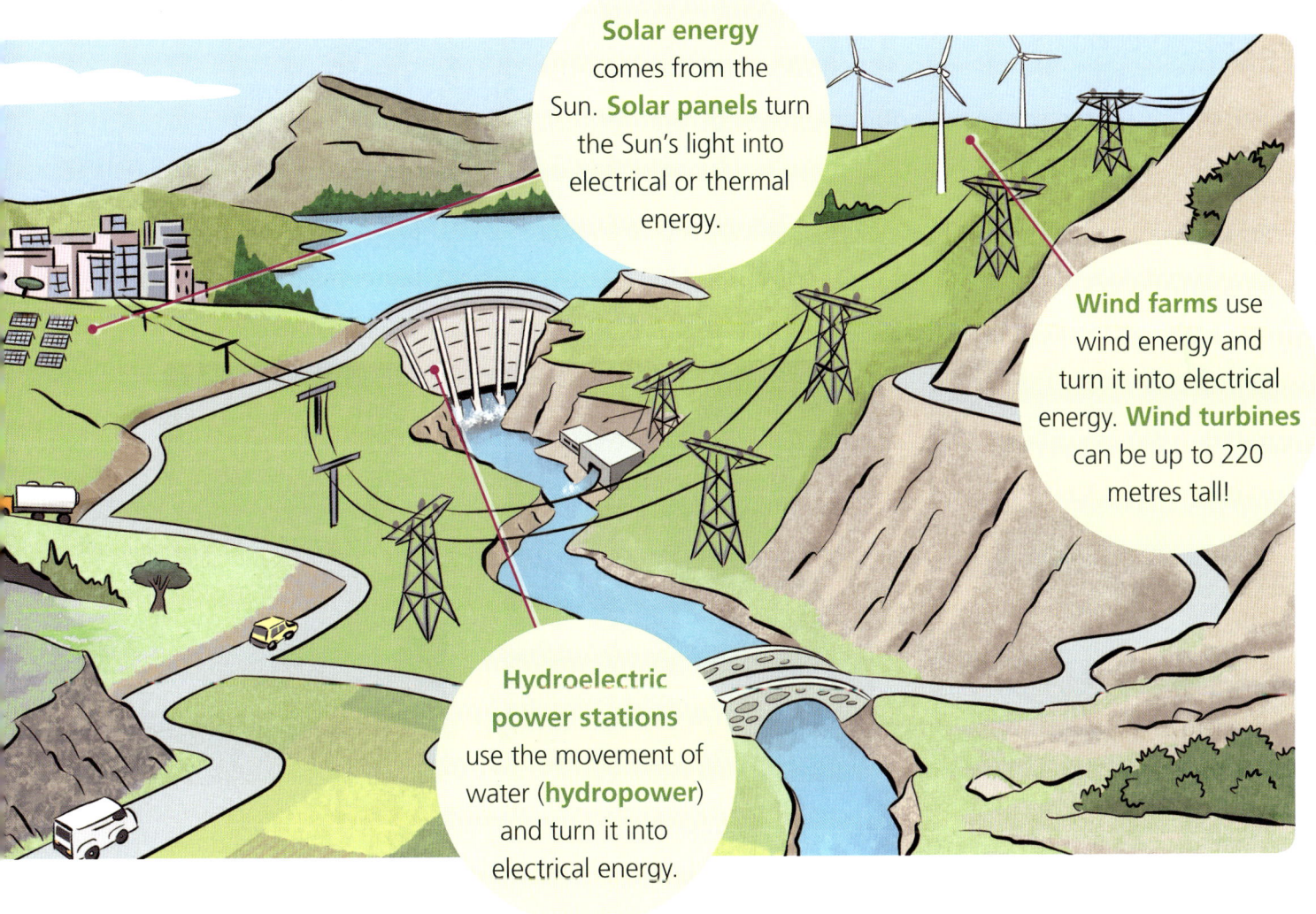

Solar energy comes from the Sun. **Solar panels** turn the Sun's light into electrical or thermal energy.

Wind farms use wind energy and turn it into electrical energy. **Wind turbines** can be up to 220 metres tall!

Hydroelectric power stations use the movement of water (**hydropower**) and turn it into electrical energy.

④ Do you think firewood is a renewable or non-renewable source of energy? Explain your ideas.

⑤ Discuss why crude oil is a very expensive energy source.

⑥ List the advantages and disadvantages of renewable energy sources.

FIND OUT: More about thermal energy

Idea:
Some materials conduct heat better than others.

- Plastic, metal and wooden spoons
- Butter
- Beans
- Hot water

Test:
Observe how some spoons conduct heat better than others.

1 Stick a bean to each spoon with butter.

2 Place the spoons in a bowl of hot water.

3 Record how quickly the butter melts on each spoon.

Conclusions

1. Which spoon conducts heat best?
2. Which spoons don't conduct heat well?
3. Lots of kitchen tools are made of wood and plastic. Discuss why.

THINK ABOUT IT: Saving energy

Saving energy isn't just about saving money. Simple actions you do every day are also good for the environment. Look at the pictures and think about how these simple actions can help us look after our planet.

a
b
c
d
e

1. Look at the pictures on the right. Where can we find these energy-saving devices? Discuss why we use these things in these places.

2. Design a comic strip to show how we can save energy every day. Think about electricity, water and heat.

LOOK BACK: Energy

Study skills

1 Copy and complete.

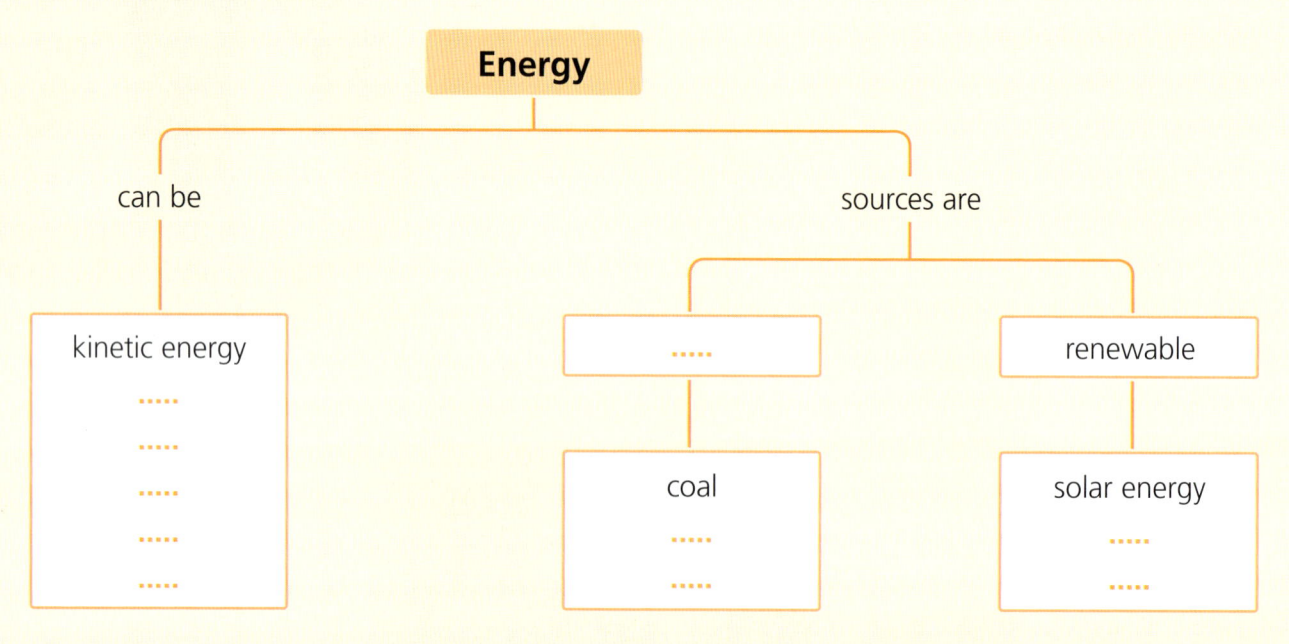

```
                    Energy
           ┌──────────┴──────────┐
         can be              sources are
           │                ┌─────┴─────┐
     kinetic energy        .....      renewable
         .....              │           │
         .....             coal     solar energy
         .....             .....       .....
         .....             .....
```

2 Make question-and-answer cards to help you revise.

- Cut out small pieces of card – about eight from one sheet of card.
- Write questions about the unit on one side of the cards.
- Write the answers on the back.
- Put the cards in a box or on the table with the questions facing up.
- Mix them up and choose a question.
- Make three piles: *correct*, *almost correct* and *wrong*.
- Keep playing until you have all of the cards in the *correct* pile.

Start today! Make question-and-answer cards to help you revise this unit.

Review

1 Unscramble the names of these common devices. Do we have to plug all of them in?

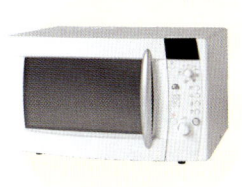

w m i c r o v a e   f e i d g r   a i o d r   w d i s h a s h r e

2 Copy and correct.

a. Cars turn kinetic energy into electrical energy.

b. When we eat food, kinetic energy is produced.

c. An oven turns light energy into thermal energy.

d. A TV turns electrical energy into light and kinetic energy.

3 Look at the pictures and say which type of energy you see.

A   B   C

4 Work in pairs. Play the true or false game.

Pupil A

a. When we move, we use kinetic energy.

b. Wind energy is a renewable energy source.

c. Solar panels turn thermal energy into kinetic energy.

Pupil B

a. We mine oil from the ground.

b. The movement of water is a source of thermal energy.

c. Firewood is a non-renewable energy source.

85

Picture dictionary

Living and non-living things

Living things

Animals are living things.

Plants are living things.

Fungi, algae and bacteria are living things.

Non-living things

natural

man-made

Matter and energy

Properties of matter

| resistant |  rigid |  rough |  fragile |

| flexible |  smooth |  waterproof |  absorbent |

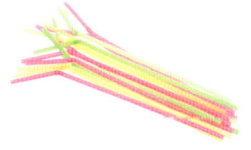

Natural and manufactured

Natural materials come from living things or from the ground.

Manufactured materials are processed from natural materials or chemicals.

Types of energy

| thermal |  kinetic |  light |

| electrical |   sound |  chemical |

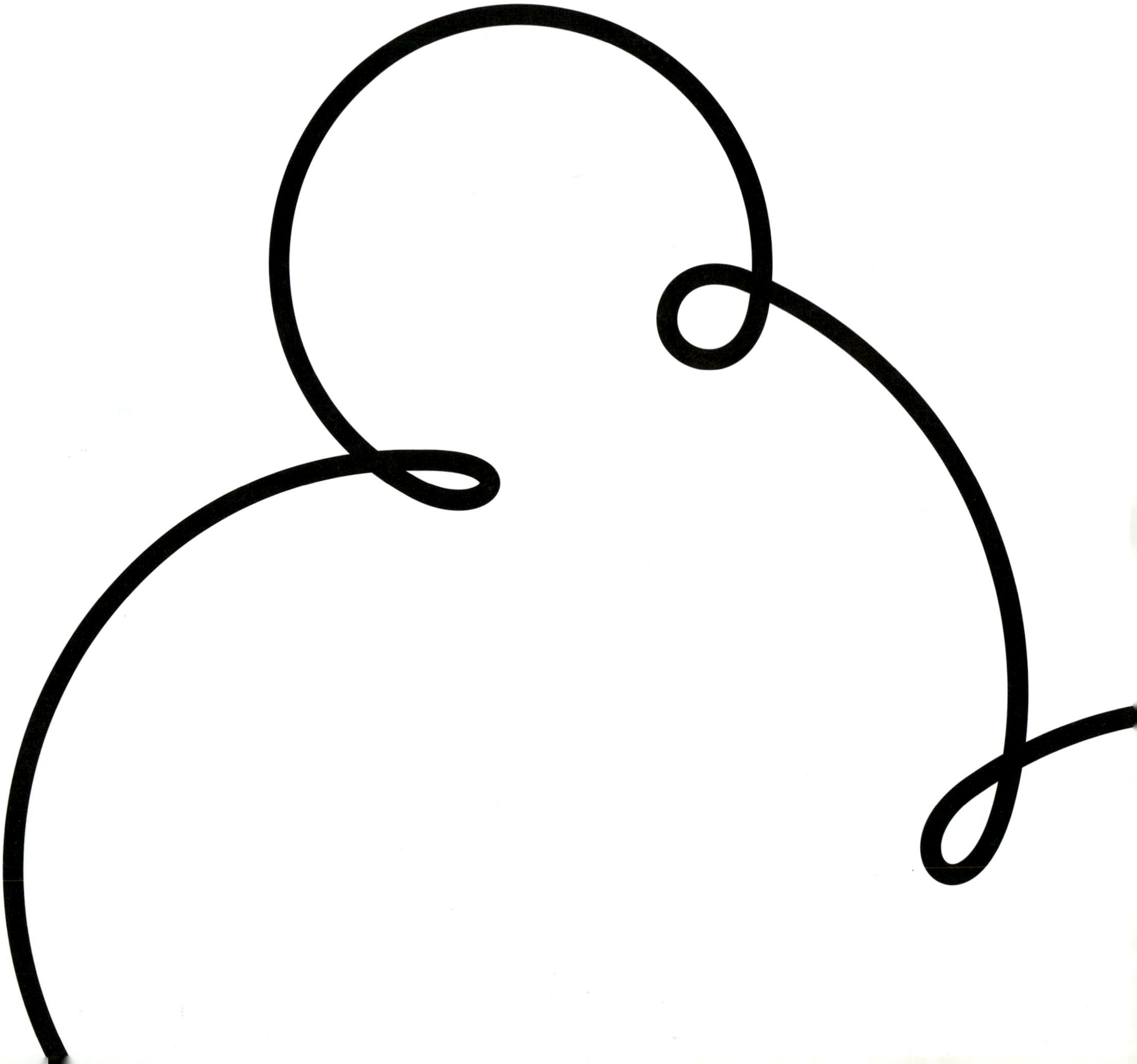